THE VULNERABILITY THESIS

THE VULNERABILITY THESIS

Interest Group
Influence and
Institutional Design

Lorelei K.
Moosbrugger

Yale UNIVERSITY PRESS
New Haven & London

Published with assistance from the foundation established in memory of Henry Weldon Barnes of the Class of 1882, Yale College.

Yale University Press books may be purchased in quantity for educational, business, or promotional use. For information, please e-mail sales.press@yale.edu (U.S. office) or sales@yaleup.co.uk (U.K. office).

Set in Galliard Old Style and Copperplate 33 types by IDS Infotech, Ltd. Printed in the United States of America.

Library of Congress Cataloging-in-Publication Data

Moosbrugger, Lorelei K.
The vulnerability thesis : interest group influence and institutional design / Lorelei K. Moosbrugger.
    p.cm.
Includes bibliographical references and index.
ISBN 978-0-300-16679-8 (pbk. : alk. paper) 1. Pressure groups. 2. Majorities. 3. Representative government and representation. 4. Pressure groups—Case studies. 5. Majorities—Case studies. 6. Representative government and representation—Case studies. I. Title.
JF529.M66 2012
322.4'3—dc23

                                        2011046003

A catalogue record for this book is available from the British Library.

This paper meets the requirements of ANSI/NISO Z39.481-992 (Permanence of Paper).

10 9 8 7 6 5 4 3 2 1

IN MEMORY OF MY FATHER,
THOMAS M. PHILLIPS

AND FOR MY SON
ALEXANDER

CARPE DIEM

CONTENTS

PREFACE

At no time since the founding of the United States have we so openly considered the effects of political institutions on the quality of democracy. In a series of eighty-five articles, the Federalist Papers focused our attention on the critical concerns of institutional design. In Federalist No.10, generally regarded as the most important of *The Federalist Papers*, Madison argued that chief among those concerns was the potentially destructive force of faction:

> Among the numerous advantages promised by a well constructed Union, none deserves to be more accurately developed than its tendency to break and control the violence of faction. By a faction, I understand a number of citizens, whether amounting to a majority or a minority of the whole, who are united and actuated by some common impulse of passion, or of interest, adversed to the rights of other citizens, or to the permanent and aggregate interests of the community.

While Madison recognized that we could not control the causes of faction without stifling political freedom, he believed we could control its effects. Minority factions, in his view, would not constitute a threat under any form of popular government because a majority would defeat the "sinister views" of a minority with the vote. Majority factions, on the other hand, are inherently dangerous because "when a majority is included in a faction, the form of popular government . . . enables it to sacrifice to its ruling passion or interest both the public good and the rights of other citizens" (*Federalist Papers,* no. 10).

To minimize the threat, Madison argued for a republic large enough to encompass a diverse electorate. He reasoned that "the smaller the society, the fewer probably will be the distinct parties and interests composing it; the fewer the distinct parties and interests, the more frequently will a majority be found of the same party. . . . Extend the sphere, and you take in a greater variety of parties and interests; you make it less probable that a majority of the whole will have a common motive to invade the rights of other citizens" (*Federalist Papers,* no. 10).

The task of institutional design was to harness the self interest of these "distinct interests and parties" to make ambition counter ambition (*Federalist Papers,* no. 51). Toward that end, Madison argued for a federal structure and a presidential executive that would divide power between independent political bodies, each of which represented distinct segments of society. He presumed that multiple centers of political authority would preserve and reflect the diversity of a large polity, safeguard individual and minority rights, and reduce the likelihood that majority factions would form adverse to the aggregate interests of the community.

Yet any observer of American politics knows that factions, or "interest groups," as they are called today, pose as much of threat to the public good now as they did in Madison's day. Ironically, most scholars of American government locate the source of interest group influence in presidentialism and federalism, the institutions designed explicitly to protect minorities and the pubic interest from the violence of faction. The lack of party discipline inherent in presidentialism is blamed for a litany of ills attributed to interest group influence in the United States, including governments' inability to provide for the health of the citizenry and their unwillingness to limit carbon emissions linked to climate change. Federalism is vilified as well, argued to be responsible for the particularistic behavior and competing ambitions of senators who seek benefits for organized groups within their local constituencies, regardless of the public costs imposed on the national polity.

The one part of the U.S. system revered for its ability to represent the majority will is the electoral system. While the single-member district (SMD) system is widely recognized as inferior to proportional representation when it comes to minority representation, it takes no blame for the undue influence of minorities or organized groups. This book was written to challenge that assumption. The theory and evidence presented here locate the source of interest group influence squarely in SMD competition and, unsurprisingly, in the resulting concentration of power in single party majorities that Madison hoped to avoid.

The case cannot be made by studying the influence of interest groups in the United States alone. Presidentialism and federalism complicate the institutional environment theoretically because they empower multiple, independent political bodies purposely designed to thwart the majority's ability to enact policies adverse to the rights of minorities. The power of interest groups may, therefore, be a legitimate by-product of institutions essential to minority representation and individual freedom. Empirically the problem is immeasurably worse. The important role of private money in American political campaigns suggests to some that the political power of organized groups in the United States is unusual. The enormous sums of money spent to contest U.S. elections, tens of millions of dollars for the most expensive House and Senate seats, and over one billion dollars for the presidency, draw our attention to the unseemly relationship between money and politics like a car accident we pass on the highway. The diversion is an equally dangerous distraction. Campaign finance laws are a political choice. The influence of private money is a symptom of the problem, not the problem itself.

Theoretically, no single case study can assess the independent role of formal political institutions on interest group capacity to influence policy choice. To identify the institutional determinants of interest group influence we must take a comparative approach that allows us to parse the individual impact of key institutions. If the electoral system is the source of interest group influence in the United States, we will find it to be the source in other states as well, even those not burdened with a presidential executive, a federal division of power, or private funding of political campaigns.

Four books were most influential on my thinking about institutions, the behavior of interest groups, and the incentives that emanate from electoral design. Together they serve as the pillars of the vulnerability thesis introduced here. David Mayhew's argument that politicians' proximate goal must be to win elections (*Congress: The Electoral Connection,* 1974) serves as a cornerstone of the logic. Arend Lijphart's seminal work in *Democracies* (1984) grounds the institutional theory, defining the critical institutional differences between states. The implications of Mancur Olson's "logic of collective action" as described in the *Rise and Decline of Nations* (1982) motivates my expectations for interest group behavior. Finally, R. Douglas Arnold's work in *The Logic of Congressional Action* (1990) informs the causal mechanisms key to the theory: identifiability and accountability. I am grateful to Yale University Press for each of these seminal publications and for allowing this work to follow in their footsteps.

I am deeply indebted to many individuals and organizations for supporting this work. Most significant is Arend Lijphart, my mentor and the single most influential individual on my thinking about how institutions work and how they affect the quality of democracy. The other political scientists on my doctoral committee constitute an embarrassment of riches to which no work could do justice. Matthew Sorberg Shugart, Kaare Strøm, and Gary Jacobson provided the early support necessary to the development of a new institutional theory. I would also like to thank Kathleen Bruhn, Laurie Freeman, Allen Hicken, Philip Roeder, and anonymous reviewers provided thoughtful feedback and constructive criticism that improved the work immeasurably. Given the shoulders on which I stand, any mistakes or errors in the logic linking interest group influence to institutional design cannot help but be mine and mine alone.

Funding provided by a Fulbright Grant to the European Union, the MacArthur Foundation, the Institute on Global Conflict and Cooperation, and the Institute for the Study of World Politics gave me access to the people and organizations necessary to investigate and test the thesis in a multitude of offices, restaurants, homes, and farms across Europe. Through my Fulbright-sponsored affiliation with the Centre for European Policy Studies, I was also able to participate in working groups and political discussion forums with a diverse group of policy makers and interested groups.

Finally, I would like to thank my husband, Daniel, for his patience, his understanding, and his excellent coffee. Without him this book would not have been possible.

THE VULNERABILITY THESIS

1

INTEREST GROUP INFLUENCE AND
INSTITUTIONAL DESIGN

... the "problem" of contemporary interest group politics is one of representation. For particular interests, especially those that are well defined and adequately funded, the government is responsive on the issues of their greatest concern. But representation is not just a matter of responding to specific interests or citizens; the government also must respond to the collective needs of society, and here the success of individual interests may *foreclose* the possibility of overall responsiveness.
—Loomis and Cigler, *Interest Group Politics*, 24 (emphasis added)

Free societies cannot prevent interest groups from making demands on government, nor would they want to. Interest groups are a natural product of political freedom and are as essential as voters to democracy. Interest groups also perform important representative functions in democratic polities. They provide voters a medium for civic engagement, they facilitate the articulation of intense societal preferences, and they provide policy makers with a breadth and depth of expertise invaluable to effective policy making. The question is, as Loomis and Cigler suggest, can political responsiveness to the specific preferences of organized groups foreclose government responsiveness to the collective needs of society?

Our understanding of collective action dynamics suggests that it can. According to Olson, although it is rational for members of small groups to organize and pursue their policy goals, it is irrational for members of large groups to organize to oppose interest group initiatives.[1] Consequently, large groups fail to mobilize against small groups' raids on the public purse, even where majorities would clearly benefit from a collective response. As a result, we expect that politicians will grant interest group benefits at public expense, and groups with a vested interest in the status quo will attempt to use their political power to inhibit policy changes that affect them adversely, even changes essential to growth. Moreover, and most important to the question at hand, the collective action advantages of organized interests may inhibit governments' ability to provide public goods if policy change will impose concentrated costs on those groups.[2]

Interest Group Influence and Institutional Design

While collective action dynamics may be universal, the political environments in which groups act vary considerably. Olson anticipated significant cross-national differences in both the demands of interest groups, i.e., the extent to which demands impose public costs for private gain, and the preferences of the political parties who respond to those demands. Small interest groups are expected to press relatively narrow demands on the state because it is rational for small groups to seek private benefits at public expense. Larger, more encompassing groups are expected to make comparatively few demands for concentrated benefits because the members of large groups will collectively bear a large portion of the public costs of interest group gain. The logic suggests similar calculations by political parties. Small parties are expected to have relatively narrow policy preferences because small political parties represent narrow constituencies. Large political parties are, by contrast, expected to advance policies that convey benefits to the large political constituencies they represent.[3]

Political scientists who study preferences have long echoed Olson's expectations, adding that it is more efficient for large parties to produce public rather than private goods to meet the demands of their broad constituencies.[4] Institutional theorists who focus on electoral incentives point out that large parties are also held accountable by electoral majorities. The reason is that large parties are normally the product of single-member district (SMD) elections and consequently ultimate policy-making power depends on maintaining a plurality, if not majority, support at the polls. Those who study policy-making dynamics note that political systems dominated by large parties also limit the number of political actors involved in policy choice and therein the number of "veto opportunities" for interest groups to influence policy makers to thwart policy change. Therefore, scholars anticipate that large parties will prefer policies that distribute benefits widely, they will be held accountable if they do not enact policy consistent with majority preferences, and the limited number of policy makers empowered in two-party systems will provide interest groups with few opportunities to veto policy change.

Political systems that empower multiple small parties generate the opposite dynamics on all three counts. First, small parties are expected to advance comparatively narrow policies that serve the interests of the comparatively narrow constituencies they represent. Second, multi-party systems tend to empower more political actors accountable to minorities because they tend to result from elections in multi-member districts (MMDs) that allow small political parties to win seats with as little as 5 percent of the vote. As a result, multi-party systems empower more political actors to influence policy choice and provide interest groups with multiple veto opportunities to influence policy change during the policy-making process. Thus, party preferences, electoral accountability, and veto points theory support the Olsonian expectation that, all else being equal, small parties will be more receptive to narrow interest group demands than will large parties.

The uniformity of theoretical predictions outlined above suggests that we should find systematic cross-national variance in policy outcomes depending on whether political institutions facilitate the creation of large or small political parties. And we do. Paradoxically, however, the systematic differences that we find contradict theoretical expectations. Large political parties that represent large constituencies are not associated with superior outcomes on any gauge of government performance, including macroeconomic measures (e.g., growth, inflation, or unemployment), social policies, environmental protection, or domestic security.[5] Ironically, political systems that empower *small* parties that represent minorities are consistently associated with a superior ability to provide public goods across a range of social and economic policies.[6]

The question is: why? Why are political systems dominated by large parties associated with lower levels of public goods if these systems increase government accountability to majorities and limit opportunities for small groups to veto policy choice? And why do political systems dominated by small parties accountable to narrow constituencies enact policies that arguably benefit majorities?

The Vulnerability Thesis

The theory introduced in this book suggests that our assumptions about the relationship between interest group influence and institutional design are wrong. It locates the overinfluence of organized groups not in the fragmentation of power across multiple minority parties, but in its political antithesis: the concentration of power in the majority. The argument in a nutshell is this: the source of interest group power is not in the representation or formal veto power of small groups, but in the vulnerability of individual politicians to retribution by organized groups. Vulnerability is greatest in political systems that concentrate power in the majority because the institutions that facilitate majority rule also make policy makers identifiable and accountable for their choices. Politicians are, by contrast, relatively invulnerable to pressure groups where institutions engender the representation of minority parties because these institutions also obscure responsibility for policy choice and limit electoral accountability, therein inhibiting political retribution by organized groups.

The argument may be counterintuitive, but the logic is straightforward. Large parties normally control the reins of political power only if they command a plurality of the vote. In countries where two large parties alternate in power, small groups wield disproportional power because a shift in electoral support of only a few percentage points often determines which party will rule. In political systems where many smaller parties compete, political power is less tied to small shifts in vote share. The reason is that governments comprised of or supported by small parties must form coalitions to pass legislation. Political power in these cases rests primarily on a party's ideological position relative to other parties, not its size. It is therefore reasonable to expect that large parties will be more vulnerable to the demands of organized groups because they can lose all political power with the small shifts in vote share that interest groups may be able to sway.

Nevertheless, the thesis is likely to generate controversy. Even scholars of comparative institutions who extol the merits of multi-party systems in terms of minority representation applaud two-party systems because they facilitate identifiability and accountability, allowing electoral majorities to "throw the rascals out."[7] Yet collective action asymmetries suggest that the identifiability and accountability that are heralded for advancing and protecting majority interests in theory may in practice be better used by small groups who seek narrow benefits at the majority's expense. The problem is that the vast majority of voters are not attentive to policy making or to the details of policy choice; nor are they likely to act to oppose interest group gains.[8] Moreover, those voters who are attentive to policy making are unlikely to punish politicians who acquiesce to interest group demands because the most politically informed are the least likely to switch parties where two large parties compete for power.[9] As a result, representatives empowered by institutions that promote majority rule must in reality be quite sensitive to *minority* opinion, especially the opinion of organized groups attentive to policy choice.[10]

The corollary expectation is likely to be more controversial. The same logic that links interest group influence to majority rule suggests that societal majorities will be advantaged in political systems that empower small parties that formally represent electoral minorities. Again, the issue is how institutions affect identifiability and accountability. The same electoral systems that allow minorities to empower small political parties ironically make these parties relatively invulnerable to retribution by small groups. As a result, institutions that facilitate the representation of minorities may also insulate governments that seek to legislate in the public interest against the excessive influence of organized groups.

Setting the Stage

This chapter lays the foundation for the development of a new, vulnerability-based theory of interest group influence in democratic countries. The process is divided into three parts. We begin with an overview of conventional theoretical expectations regarding the relative power of groups under different institutional designs. The objective of the review is to provide the reader with the necessary background to compare and contrast the expectations of the vulnerability thesis with those of existing institutional theories. The second section specifies the requisites of a research design capable of testing competing theories of interest group influence on policy choice. We then preview the case study chosen for the first crucial test of the theory, comparative agrochemical policy. The chapter concludes with a discussion of the implications of the vulnerability-based model for our understanding of interest group influence and institutional design.

Institutional Theory: Minority Influence and Majority Rule

Majorities are ultimately responsible for policy choice in all democratic countries, regardless of institutional stripe. Institutional models that explain the policy influence of small groups must therefore explain how minorities can influence policy ultimately made by representatives of the majority. The models that dominate our understanding of interest group influence during policy making originated with Ellen Immergut's (1990) introduction of the veto points paradigm. The basic theory is that the political power of interest groups will reflect the number of "veto points" in the decision-making process, i.e., institutionalized opportunities for small groups to influence policy makers to "veto" proposed changes to the status quo in the decision-making process.

Veto-based theories classify a large number of important institutions; however, the three primary institutional determinants of the number of veto points in democratic systems are the executive regime (presidential or parliamentary), the number of legislative bodies (unicameral or bicameral), and the number of political parties that must agree to policy change (multiparty coalitions or a single majority party). We review each of these below.

AUTHORITY AND DISCIPLINE IN EXECUTIVE REGIMES A key expectation of veto-based theories is that parliamentary regimes will offer interest groups fewer opportunities to influence policy choice than will presidential regimes. In parliamentary regimes the executive is derived from the legislature and it is the locus of new policy proposals. In addition, both bodies are "disciplined" by the fact that their origins and survival are fused. Origins affect the use of legislative vetoes because parliamentary executives begin their tenures with a certain minimum of parliamentary support to enact policy change. Fused survival also affects policy making. While parliamentary legislatures normally have the power to vote "no confidence" in the government, prime ministerial authority to dismiss the legislature if it does not support critical bills inhibits legislative vetoes during the term. Scholars argue that the centralization of policy-making authority and the strong party discipline that parliamentary government engenders insulate parliamentary executives from interest group influence, allowing them to impose concentrated costs on organized groups when necessary for the provision of public goods.[11]

In contrast, presidential regimes empower two independent political bodies, an executive and a legislature, each with the authority to veto policy change. The division of power between two independent political bodies provides interest groups with at least two opportunities to affect policy choice, one via the majority party(ies) in the legislature, and another through the executive.[12] Presidentialism also reduces incentives for party discipline, which makes each individual legislator a potential veto opportunity. Unlike prime ministers, presidents cannot normally dismiss the legislature and therefore, unlike members of parliament, individual legislators do not need to toe the party line to remain in power. Consequently, legislators in presidential systems are not insulated from interest group demands by the dictates of the party leadership, even when they belong to the same party as the president. Therefore veto-based theories anticipate that legislators in presidential regimes may be vulnerable to the demands of small groups within their individual constituencies, even if those demands subvert their party's ability to provide public goods to national constituencies.[13]

Despite the intellectual appeal of theoretical predictions, there is no comparative evidence to support this core expectation. As intuitive as it may be, cross-national differences in policy choice do not suggest that parliamentary regimes have a superior capacity to impose costs on interest groups or provide public goods to broad constituencies. In Weaver and Rockman's edited volume devoted to assessing the empirical evidence for policy variance resulting from the presidential-parliamentary distinction, none of the ten case studies demonstrate that parliamentary executives enjoy a superior capacity to imposed concentrated costs or enact policy change. To quote Feigenbaum, Samuels, and Weaver in their chapter, "The distinction between parliamentary systems and the U.S. separation-of-powers systems does not go very far in explaining institutional capabilities." Weaver and Rockman ultimately find that "the U.S. system does not stand out from all parliamentary systems in its patterns of capabilities, but rather tends to cluster with the coalitional systems on many of those capabilities." The authors conclude that the institutional dynamics are complex, and that other institutional variables often intervene to influence outcomes.[14]

THE DIVISION OF POWER BETWEEN INDEPENDENT LEGISLATIVE BODIES A second major institutional distinction examined by veto point theorists is that between unicameral and bicameral legislatures. Here scholars expect that cross-national differences in government capacity to impose geographically concentrated costs will reflect systematic differences in the formal representation of subnational constituencies. Just as a legislative majority has the power to veto executive proposals and thwart policy agendas in presidential regimes, the second legislative chambers necessitated by federalism can generally veto policies made by bare majorities in the popularly elected assembly. Consequently, even single-party majority executives in parliamentary systems may be forced to compromise with representatives of electoral minorities if a federal division of power creates a bicameral legislature.

We expect federalism to advantage geographically concentrated interest groups because politicians who represent subnational interests are explicitly empowered to advance policies that benefit geographic minorities and obstruct policy changes that impose concentrated costs on those minorities.[15] An additional legislative body necessarily generates additional veto players as well, veto players that are likely to impede governments' ability to make policy efficiently (without compromise) because they hold substantively different priorities than those of the executive or popularly elected assembly.

Surprisingly however, while many studies attempt to measure the effect of state structure on government performance, none provide evidence to suggest that unitary systems are categorically superior to federal systems in resisting the demands of subnational minorities. While federal systems are associated with systematic differences in policy outcomes, namely greater private investment, lower government spending, and smaller public sectors, the linkage between federalism and these outcomes is obscured by several other variables.

Researchers find that the ideological complexion of government, the interest group system, and the independence of central banks explain much more cross-national variance in the policy outcomes associated with federalism than the difference between state structures.[16] Central bank independence is an especially complicating variable empirically. The correlation between federalism and central bank independence is so strong that Lijphart includes it among the institutions that define the federal-unitary dimension of the majoritarian-consensual distinction, the dominant paradigm used to classify democratic institutions.[17] Another complicating factor is that the interest group system and the ideological complexion of government are empirically correlated with the electoral system.[18] Consequently the complexity of the institutional environment precludes linking federalism directly to minority influence or cross-national differences in policy choice.

MINORITY REPRESENTATION VIA POLITICAL PARTIES Immergut's veto points paradigm was followed closely by a separate, more general theory of "veto players" that suggests that the number of political parties included in policy making will also affect interest groups' opportunities to thwart policy change.[19] Unlike Immergut's conception of veto points as existing outside the executive, the veto players' model anticipates that parties within executive coalitions may veto policy proposals that would impose costs on their constituencies.[20]

Yet as discussed above, political systems dominated by small parties regularly enact policy changes that provide superior public goods across the policy spectrum. Scholars have offered a number of explanations for the observed differences in policy choice, the most important of which can be organized into two main groups: interactive models that focus on party preferences and government capacity, and formal models that focus on incentives deriving from district size. The interactive models depict policy choice as a product of what governments want and their ability to enact those policies without interference. The district-size models depict policy choice as a product of what rank-and-file representatives need to deliver to their individual constituencies to remain in power. Both rely on the key premise of veto points models, namely that policy outcomes reflect the preferences of policy makers' empowered to veto policy change—and by extension the groups to which they owe their elections. The fundamental assumptions and expectations of each are described briefly below.

INTERACTIVE MODELS: COLLECTIVE RESPONSIBILITY AND CONCENTRATED AUTHORITY Two important models suggest that government provision of broad-based public goods is a product of institutional *combinations* that 1) facilitate the representation of a broad group of ideological minorities (via multiple political parties) *and* 2) concentrate policy-making authority in a single political body (i.e., a unicameral parliament).[21] Birchfield and Crepaz's (1998) model of "collective" and "competitive" veto points posits that institutional designs that divide policy-making power among multiple political parties *and* concentrate authority in a parliamentary executive create veto points that generate incentives for decision makers to act collectively. By contrast, institutional combinations that divide political authority between two or more independent political bodies (via presidentialism and/or federalism) but concentrate political power in a single "majority" party create veto points that generate incentives for parties to act competitively. As a result, the authors anticipate qualitatively different policy outcomes in these two specific political systems. They expect that collective veto players will refrain from using their individual vetoes in order to produce public goods available to their collectively broad constituencies. Competitive veto players, by contrast, are expected to use their institutional vetoes to inhibit policy change when it affects their constituencies negatively.

The "Centripetal Theory of Democratic Governance" introduced by Gerring, Thacker, and Moreno (2005) and later developed by Gerring and Thacker (2008) associates the same institutional combinations with the same general outcomes, but via a (slightly) different causal mechanism. The authors argue that the different routes to representation generate different "forces" on policy making. They posit that the combination of proportional representation (PR) elections, unicameral legislatures, and parliamentary executive regimes generate centripetal forces on policy making that foster government responsibility to national constituencies. SMD elections, presidentialism, and federalism, by contrast, generate centrifugal forces on policy making, dividing responsibility between independent bodies at the national level and between national and subnational interests. Centrifugal forces inhibit government provision of public goods targeted at broad national constituencies.

While the two interactive models differ theoretically, they generate identical expectations empirically. Multi-party parliamentary executives in unitary states are depicted as most likely to provide broad-based public goods; two-party systems that empower presidential executives in federal states are depicted as the least likely to advocate those policies. Importantly, however, neither interactive model predicts policy-making in political systems that are not defined by these specific institutional combinations. Consequently, neither can explain why institutional designs that empower single-party majority governments that do not have to compromise with veto players in other political bodies (i.e., majority parties in unicameral parliamentary executives) also fail to enact policies that provide public goods to their necessarily broad, national constituencies. Both also fail to explain why small parties that wield a veto in national policy making choose not to use their veto to protect their minority, albeit national constituencies.

DISTRICT-SIZE MODELS: ELECTORAL DRIVEN INCENTIVES Models based on electoral incentives associated with district size shift the analytical focus from the incentives that face parties in government to those that face representatives from individual districts. They suggest that large parties who compete in small, SMD elections face incentives to allow their individual representatives to bring home targeted district benefits. By contrast, the small parties that compete in large MMDs face incentives to provide society-wide, group-based benefits available to voters who reside in districts across the country.[22]

The logic of district-based models is not inconsistent with Gerring et al.'s centripetal theory of democratic governance. District-based models suggest that SMD competition will generate incentives for parties to respond to subnational preferences more than to national preferences, which is arguably a "centrifugal force." Policymaking by multiple small parties will, by contrast, generate incentives for small parties to forge policy-making coalitions at the national level, which is arguably a "centripetal force." The logic is also consistent with Birchfield and Crepaz's model, which differentiates interactor dynamics associated with "collective" and "competitive" veto points. It suggests in fact that the competitive forces not fully explained by the model may reflect geographically based competition for national resources.

District-based models are, however, in direct contrast to veto-based expectations for cross-system difference in parliamentary and presidential regimes because the district-based logic suggests that large parties in parliamentary regimes make policy based on the electoral needs of its individual members, not on the collective needs of the party.[23] The logic is also at odds with decades of research in the party-system literature, all of which depicts single-party majority governments in parliamentary regimes as characterized by strong party discipline. In fact, the logic would force us to reject the long-held belief that parliamentary governments led by majority parties are comparatively the most "responsible" to the national polity.

More important, district-based models cannot explain why small parties do not use their veto to protect minority constituencies. This is a critical failing. The costs associated with the provision of broad-based public goods necessarily fall more on some groups than on others, be it higher-income taxpayers or regulated enterprises. And as the collective action literature accurately predicts, affected groups are attentive to these policy choices and are likely to act to oppose the costs of policy change. Therefore the challenge for institutional theorists is not to explain how politicians or the parties to which they belong provide private benefits or public goods, but instead to explain how politicians and parties impose concentrated costs on constituent groups. Yet none of the theories discussed above can identify the institutional configurations under which such cost imposition occurs.

BRINGING INTEREST GROUPS INTO THE ANALYSIS To expect existing institutional theories to explain interest group influence may be to expect too much. Institutional theory functions much like a streetlight, focusing our attention on the dynamics it illuminates. Therefore we look to execu-tive authority, the size of political constituencies, or the number of political actors included in policy choice to explain relationships between interest groups and politicians because these variables explain how institutions shape politicians' incentives to represent groups during policy making. Questions about politicians' relationships with interest groups require a different approach; we need to illuminate a different part of the political game.

The vulnerability thesis developed in the following chapter shifts our theoretical focus from the policies preferred by represented groups to the choices politically tenable for politicians who seek reelection. It argues that the key to government provision of public goods is not that the small parties that represent minority interests collectively prefer those goods, but that small parties can provide those goods *against* the preferences of organized groups within their core constituencies.

The causal mechanism that links the size and number of parties to cross-national differences in policy choice is political vulnerability to retribution. The thesis is based on the simple proposition that organized groups will be most powerful where they can identify policy makers responsible for policy choices, and voters can hold politicians accountable for those choices at the polls. It anticipates that interest groups will be least powerful where they cannot identify those responsible for policy choice or where politicians are unlikely to be removed from power with the small shifts in vote share that interest groups can sway.

Unlike veto-based models that focus our attention on the concentration of power in the executive or assign equal importance to all institutions that affect the number of veto players, the vulnerability thesis identifies the electoral system as the critical institution linked to interest group power. SMD elections make politicians most vulnerable because they maximize identifiability and accountability regardless of executive regime or the internal division of power. Contrary to conventional wisdom, multi-member systems, especially those that use PR, are posited to minimize vulnerability because they obscure identifiability and inhibit electoral accountability. Hierarchically defined institutional combinations are placed on a continuum of political vulnerability that ranks the vulnerability of policy makers in all democracies regardless of the institutional design. The relative ranking of political systems argues against the long-held belief that parliamentary regimes are categorically superior to presidential systems, positing instead that parliamentary and presidential systems can be more or less vulnerable to the demands of small groups, depending on the number of parties in the party system. The thesis also argues against those who anticipate a significant effect from state structure because the internal division of power is not an important predictor of system vulnerability.

Testing the Thesis: The Requisites of Research Design

The first section of chapter three identifies the conditions necessary to conduct a decisive test of the model. Given the regularity with which political observers point to interest group influence on policy choice, one might expect that it would be fairly easy to identify a policy area offering a clear cross-national test of the model. In fact, it is not. The problem is that cross-national differences in policy choice may reflect cross-national differences in government ideology or the system of interest group representation, and both variables tend to co-vary with the electoral system.

Electoral Systems, Government Ideology, and Corporatism

Research shows that political systems that use PR elections are normally governed by parties of the left; political systems that use SMD elections are, by contrast, normally governed by parties of the right.[24] As a result, the institution argued to be at the source of politicians' vulnerability to interest group demands is strongly correlated with the ideological complexion of government. This is important because some argue that the relative desirability of public goods, especially those that demand high levels of taxation and government spending, is a normative question, one with deep roots in culture and ideology.[25] These models suggest that low taxes and concomitantly low levels of government services in countries with SMD rules and large political parties reflect their British heritage of a liberal ideology rather than their use of the British electoral system. Consequently, it is reasonable to argue that cross-national differences in social policies, income inequality, and tax rates (for example) may reflect real differences in the ideological preferences of governments and the publics they serve. Therefore case selection must ensure that variance in interest group influence cannot be attributed to ideological preferences, especially regarding the proper role of government in the economy.

Cross-national differences in the system of interest group representation present a similar challenge. Pluralist systems of interest group representation are generally found in countries using SMD electoral systems, while corporatism is normally associated with countries that use PR elections.[26] Like the relationship between federalism and central bank independence, the correlation between the electoral system and interest group system is so strong that Lijphart includes the interest group system among the institutions that differentiate the majoritarian-consensual distinction. Consequently, like SMD elections, two-party systems and single-party majority governments, pluralism is one of the institutions that define majoritarian systems. Similarly, corporatism is included among PR elections, multi-party systems, and coalition governments as one of the institutions that define consensual systems.

More important, scholars have posited a causal relationship between cross-national differences in the system of interest group representation, the electoral system, and policy choice. Recall that Olson (1965, 1982) expected the size of the interest group to affect the group's policy prefer-ences. Unorganized pluralist interest group systems are characterized by a multiplicity of small groups, each making its own narrow claims on the state. Highly organized and regulated corporatism systems, by contrast, are characterized by a small number of large, hierarchically ordered groups that tend to make broad claims on the state that benefit large memberships. Katzenstein (1985) argues that PR facilitated the adoption of corporatist interest group systems, and that corporatism explains economic policy choice in PR countries. Crepaz and Lijphart (1991) also argue that corpo-ratism is associated with PR, and they associate PR and corporatism with the superior provision of some public goods in particular.[27] Gerring, Thacker, and Moreno (2005) and Gerring and Thacker (2008) are most explicit in linking corporatism to the superior provision of public goods generally, identifying corporatism as one of the intermediate variables that link PR to distinct patterns of policy choice.

Given that corporatist systems both empower labor groups and insti-tutionalize interest groups' cooperation with the state, it is not surprising that corporatism is associated with an activist state and benefits for working people, including government-provided health care and labor rights. Consequently, policies that are the purview of corporatist actors are vulnerable to the same problem associated with ideologically linked policies discussed above; the source of policy variance cannot be definitively determined. Therefore, the characteristics that differentiate interest groups in pluralist and corporatist systems, i.e., the size of interest groups, the inclusion of groups during policy making, and the need to compromise with structured opposition, must also be made equal through research design.

The methodological need to avoid ideologically tainted policies and those likely to reflect cross-national differences in the system of interest group representation argues against a comparative analysis of many policy outcomes commonly measured in the literature. A decisive test of this—or any other institutional model—must be invulnerable to arguments that variance in policy choice can be attributed to the ideological preferences of governments or the system of interest group representation. Caution in case selection should not suggest, however, that the utility of the vulnerability thesis is limited to instances where no other explanation for cross-national differences in policy choice is possible. As will be discussed in the conclusion of this book, the vulnerability thesis offers a potentially valuable alternative explanation for cross-national differences in policy choices across the policy spectrum.

Preview: Agrochemical Policy Making

Given the considerations above, comparative trends in the use of agricultural fertilizers and pesticides offer an excellent opportunity to conduct the first crucial test of the model. While not all environmental issues are neutral with respect to ideological preferences, political parties across the ideological spectrum support environmental regulations that ensure safe drinking water and the viability of water resources. In addition, unlike other common measures of environmental quality (e.g., air quality, carbon emissions, and recycling rates), cross-national differences in resource endowments and economic structure do not directly affect pollution levels or the need for regulatory policies.

Policies that affect agriculture also allow us to control for the theoretical impacts of corporatism. Agriculture is one of few policy areas in which differences between interest group size are empirically inconsequential. In addition, agriculture has insider status in both types of interest group systems, with a demonstrated ability to shape much of the legislation that governs the agriculture industry in general.[28] Finally, unlike the competitive and "countervailing" relationship between labor and employer groups during policy making that affects workers' wages and benefits, agricultural organizations do not face structured opposition in corporatist systems.[29] As a result, the three attributes posited to differentiate interest group demands in pluralist systems from their corporatist cousins are, for these intents and purposes, equal. Therefore, an analysis of cross-national differences in agrochemical pollution allows us to assess the independent impact of institutions on the government protection of an important public good, namely water quality.

MULTI-METHOD DESIGN: QUANTITATIVE ANALYSES AND CASE STUDIES The links between formal political institutions and farmers' use of agrochemicals are not intuitive. Absent the argument made here, there is no reason to anticipate that formal political institutions will affect farmers' choices regarding the use of fertilizers and pesticides in the field. Yet researchers cannot explain cross-national variance in agrochemical use with either agricultural requisites or economic considerations, the two most reasonable explantions.[30] The policy analysis in chapter three reveals, however, that cross-national differences in chemical use do reflect systematic differences in policy choice, and those policy differences are correlated with differences in institutional designs consistent with the vulnerability thesis.

While comparative analyses are often limited to assessing differences in policy choice, the availability of decades of cross-national data on agrochemical use allows us to test the relationship between policy choice and actual environmental quality. Therefore, a "vulnerability index" is created to test the relationship between institutional design and long-term changes in agrochemical use quantitatively. The findings reveal that government structure is strongly correlated with changes in agrochemical use, statistically and substantively, controlling for changes in cropping patterns, the economic importance of agricultural and chemical sectors, and public opinion.

Nevertheless, linking farmers' use of fertilizers and pesticides to the vulnerability of policy makers is admittedly a tough sell. While the vulnerability thesis suggests that there should be a relationship, and both cross-national differences in policy choice and quantitative analysis of agrochemical use support that claim, a search for alternative explanations requires in-depth country analyses. The case studies in chapters four through eight trace historic trends in the usage of agrochemicals in conjunction with government policies in four countries: Austria, Britain, Germany, and Sweden. Limiting case studies to European countries was an essential first cut because European agricultural sectors have been subject to many of the same historical, cultural, and technological influences. These specific countries were chosen based on their ability to serve as models of the institutional differentiation posited to influence the politicians' vulnerability to interest group demands, i.e., SMD or PR electoral systems, single-party majority or multi-party coalition governments, and federal or unitary state structures. Selection of these four cases also allows us to test the efficacy of the vulnerability model vis-à-vis competing models empirically.

Britain is the only European country that fully concentrates political power in the national majority. SMD elections in a parliamentary and unitary state normally empower a single majority party with the executive capacity to govern decisively. Conventional theories suggest that this institutional configuration should insulate governments from interest group demands and therein allow them to enact majority-preferred policies. By contrast, Sweden is the prototypical case of a multi-party system empowered by PR in a parliamentary and unitary state. Political power is dispersed among multiple parties that normally cooperate to enact policy change. While Britain and Sweden are unitary systems, federalism in Germany and Austria gives substantial power to representatives of subnational interests. Germany uses a mixed-member electoral system that empowers two large parties that alternate in government but also consistently gives disproportionate political power to small parties. Austria is an important case theoretically because its PR electoral system traditionally empowered only two political parties, permitting us to tease out the role of the electoral system and government type.

These four cases also allow us to test for effects that may result from membership in the European Union (EU). While Germany and the United Kingdom have been long-standing members of the EU, Austria and Sweden became members only in 1995.[31] Although the EU is not a sovereign state and therefore not directly subject of the theoretical model tested, the EU demands analysis for two reasons. First, the EU makes some policy for its member countries much like the central government of a federal state. Moreover, the greatest influence on agricultural decisions in the member states of the EU, including the use of agrochemicals, is arguably the EU's Common Agricultural Policy. Second, the EU is emerging as an international leader in environmental policy, wielding substantial authority over environmental regulations affecting agriculture and agrochemical use. A study of European agriculture must therefore examine the potential influence of this international body on domestic choices to control for its effects. Therefore the EU is presented as the first case study.

The country case studies that follow reveal dramatic cross-national variance in government capacity to impose concentrated costs on organized groups. During the period studied (1970–1995), British farmers doubled their per hectare use of nitrogen while Swedish farmers reduced their agrochemical use by 75 percent, arguably producing the cleanest, "greenest" crops in the world. The policy histories of these two cases are as different as their results. While British governments in power during this period incurred substantial public costs to avoid imposing concentrated costs on organized groups, Swedish governments used every instrument in their arsenal to reduce usage.

Case studies of Austria and Germany are equally informative theoretically, and perhaps more instructive empirically. The governments of both countries were vulnerable to interest group demands, yet both imposed costs via indirect methods, and with surprisingly effective results. This is important because while academics are primarily concerned with understanding the institutional determinants of interest group power, the question for many governments is how to impose necessary costs on powerful groups if the system inhibits it. The case studies of Germany and Austria provide some answers.

Implications for Institutional Theory

The primary goal of this book is to offer a general model of the institutional determinants of interest group influence and demonstrate empirically that political institutions affect the ability of organized groups to subvert government provision of public goods. The most important contribution of this research, however, is in the area of democratic theory. Scholars have long argued that inherent in electoral system choice is a tradeoff between voter representation and policy-making efficiency. Electoral systems that facilitate the representation of minority parties, especially partylist PR, provide for the broadest representation of societal interests but also slow decision making by requiring compromise among multiple political parties. While electoral systems promoting majority rule necessarily limit representation of minority interests, many assume the efficient translation of majority preferences compensates for the loss. Bringing interest groups into the analysis challenges that assumption.

The vulnerability thesis suggests that SMD electoral systems, the single most important institution facilitating majority rule, will inhibit the provision of public goods when costs must be imposed on powerful groups. Electoral systems that enhance minority representation, by contrast, will enable the imposition of costs on organized interest groups and therein government provision of public goods. Under these conditions majoritarian elections will not facilitate a more efficient means to majority-preferred ends, but instead create obstacles to those ends.

As a result, the thesis contradicts the conventional wisdom on two fronts. First, the thesis argues against the almost unquestioned theoretical linkage between majoritarian elections, political accountability, and majority-preferred policies. This is important because the legitimacy of majoritarian electoral systems rests on the assumption that they facilitate political accountability to electoral majorities. Majoritarian elections are already associated with lower levels of voter participation, higher levels of political violence, inferior representation of societal minorities, less policy congruence with the median voter, and lower levels of political sophistication.[32] If these systems are also more vulnerable to interest group demands and as a result reduce politicians' capacity to produce public goods, there is little to recommend them.[33]

Second, the thesis suggests that the multi-party systems that generate higher levels of voter participation, superior representation of societal minorities, greater policy congruence with the median voter, and higher levels of political sophistication *also* shield policy makers against the demands of small, organized groups. This argues against the equally long-held, if less explicit, assumption that we trade the overinfluence of small groups for minority protections. Indeed, it indicates the opposite is true. The vulnerability thesis anticipates that the influence of electoral minorities and organized interest groups is inversely related, i.e., interest groups' influence is likely to be highest where minorities are least powerful politically, and lowest where electoral minorities are most influential. As a result, electoral institutions that facilitate the representation of societal minorities can insulate majorities against the excessive influence of organized groups. Consequently, we do not trade minority protections for interest group power; we control interest group power with minority protections.

2

THE VULNERABILITY THESIS

> In considering the veto potential of a particular interest group, one should note that the concept of interest group power itself raises some questions. Why should it be possible for members of a group like the medical profession, who, after all, constitute only a very small minority of voters, to influence the decision of politicians?
> —Immergut, *Health Politics* 1992:393

Immergut's question highlights the fundamental problem with veto-based models of interest group influence, i.e., the assumption that interest groups influence politicians via the same pathways used by voters. The reality, as we all know, is quite different. The medical profession can influence policy makers precisely because it is an organized interest group—not just a small group of voters.

Interest Groups as Unique Political Actors

The defining difference between interest groups and voters is that interest groups are organized to influence policy choice; voters are not.[1] The political activity of most voters is limited to choosing representatives from among competing parties.[2] In contrast, organized groups are not satisfied to get their preferred party elected; they want their preferred policy enacted. Consequently, interest groups are politically active between elections. Interest groups interact with the media and other organized groups, they initiate or participate in litigation, and they orchestrate citizen letter-writing and e-mail campaigns. In addition, interest groups regularly provide politicians and executive agencies with information and expertise both directly and through advisory groups and expert hearings; some even help draft regulations and proposed legislation.[3] Organized groups are therefore well informed about policy changes that may affect them, especially changes that may impose concentrated costs on the group or its members.[4]

Given their high levels of information, interest group activity is especially important during elections. Organized groups provide information to the media to influence voters to support, or to withhold their support from, candidates in response to politicians' policy positions or legislative performance.[5] Interest groups' policy positions often influence vote choice because they serve as credible heuristics for undecided voters.[6] In addition, interest groups control a variety of resources—financial, informational, and organizational—that can influence voters indirectly.[7]

As a result, politicians must be especially sensitive to how their actions affect attentive organized groups, and anticipate how interest groups will respond to their actions.[8] The question is, under what conditions does that sensitivity enhance government performance by facilitating the influence of groups with special knowledge or intense preferences, and under what conditions does that sensitivity "foreclose" the provision of public goods because politicians do not enact needed reforms that impose costs on attentive groups?

Empiricists have found it difficult to answer that question directly. In a thorough review of decades of research on the American case, Baumgartner and Leech conclude that the evidence is surprisingly inconclusive. Despite their near perpetual political activity, extensive lobbying, and direct contributions to political campaigns, it is difficult to link interest group preferences to specific policy choices. The core problem is that significant interest group influence occurs well before votes are taken on individual policy proposals. Interest groups may in fact exert their greatest influence in the form of agenda control, keeping potential policy choices from being debated. Consequently, Baumgartner and Leech conclude that we are attempting to measure the "unmeasurable."[9]

Political scientists are, therefore, in a position similar to those who study black holes; we are forced to look for evidence of interest group influence, because what we are looking for is impossible to observe directly. Consequently, we must begin with a theory; only when we know where to look can we begin to assess cross-national differences in interest group influence on policy.

The inefficacy of veto-based theories reviewed in the previous chapter suggests that we have been looking in the wrong places. This chapter introduces a new institutional theory of interest group influence, one that anticipates different cross-national patterns in policy choices. The chapter is divided into two parts. We begin by defining the vulnerability thesis, its core concepts, and the causal mechanism at work. Next we develop a model to direct empirical research based on theoretical expectations regarding institutional design. Model development concludes with the creation of a continuum of political vulnerability in democratic countries.

The Vulnerability Thesis

The vulnerability thesis is that the political power of organized groups lies in the vulnerability of individual politicians to retribution for policy choice. It is premised on the assumption that the political power of small groups is in their attentiveness to policy choice and their ability to punish politicians for choices that affect the groups adversely. It suggests therefore that the line between sensitivity and vulnerability to organized groups can be drawn between systems that allow adversely affected groups to punish politicians for policy choice and those that do not.

Political vulnerability logically rests on two necessary conditions. Politicians can be vulnerable only where political institutions 1) allow interest groups to identify the policy makers responsible for policy choice and 2) voters can remove politicians from power at the polls. Therefore identifiability and accountability play the critical roles.

Identifiability and Accountability: Defining Concepts

Political accountability can be conceptualized a number of ways.[10] As used here, it refers to politicians' direct accountability to voters. It is therefore consistent with the most traditional and least restrictive definitions, including Powell's conceptualization of elections as "instruments of control" that allow voters to remove politicians who are "doing the wrong thing" (2000:11). It is also consistent with Riker's (1982) focus on retrospective accountability, defined as voters' ability to "throw the rascals out." The relationship of primary importance is therefore that between voters and politicians who stand for election, or what Carey (2009) refers to as "individual accountability" rather than the "collective accountability" of governing parties to their supporting members of parliament.

Identifiability refers to voters' and interest groups' ability to identify those responsible for policy choice.[11] Arnold (1990) refers to a similar dynamic as "traceability." He states that traceability requires "the existence of three conditions; a perceptible effect, an identifiable governmental action, and a legislator's visible contribution." Traceability captures the intent of the concept, but cannot substitute for identifiability as defined here because identifiability does not require the first or third condition.

Powell and Whitten's (1993) "clarity of responsibility" is nearly a perfect match, and therefore merits special attention. Clarity of responsibility is a multi-faceted concept that reflects outcomes associated with multiple institutions within a single political system. The authors define clarity as a product of five factors: 1) the voting cohesion of the major governing party, 2) the degree to which legislative committees include nongovernment parties, 3) whether or not nongovernment parties control a second legislative chamber, 4) minority or majority status of governments (in parliamentary regimes), and 5) single-party or coalition governments. Each of these factors certainly affect citizens' (or interest groups') ability to identify who is responsible for policy choice, and scholars do not indicate that additional factors should be included.

Nevertheless, the clarity variable is not used here due to its complexity and its dynamic nature. Clarity of responsibility as defined above requires that one know which parties are in government, the distribution of their support in the legislature, whether or not one or more nongovernment parties control a second chamber, and the extent to which the rank and file vote with the party leadership. The goal of this work is to create a general model of politicians' vulnerability to interest group influence that ranks democratic political systems on a continuum that is independent of distribution of power among parties. Therefore, the relative placement of individual political systems cannot depend on the particular distribution of partisan support during any one administration. Note, however, that identifiability is ultimately defined by the electoral system and division of power between independent political bodies, institutions that affect four of the five component measures of Powell and Whitten's concept of "clarity of responsibility."

Causal Mechanisms

Identifiability has already been linked to interest group influence on policy choice. In *The Logic of Congressional Action* (1990), Arnold argues that interest groups' ability to identify individuals responsible for policy choice can inhibit government capacity to impose concentrated costs and produce public goods. The problem results from asymmetries for collective action: politicians are more responsive to attentive groups, small or large, than they are to inattentive groups.[12] As a result, Arnold argues that the identity of decision makers must be hidden from those who will suffer the private costs of policy change—even change that benefits a majority of voters. Where the identifiability of individual policy makers cannot be obscured, policies must be either imposed by a third party or included in omnibus legislation.[13] Like Arnold, Wicksell ([1886] 1967) also prescribed omnibus legislation as a method to produce public goods. Krehbiel (1991) argues instead for restrictive rules to preclude floor amendments in the U.S. Congress, but for the same reason.[14]

Accountability has also been linked to interest group influence. Weaver and Rockman argue that "the problem of the U.S. system is not so much that accountability is lacking, but rather that it is divided and targeted effectively at individual politicians" (1993:460). Pierson and Weaver generalize, stating that "governmental capabilities for loss imposition depend largely on concentrating power and diffusing or limiting accountability for those actions" (1993:144). Therefore it is not unreasonable (or even novel) to suggest that the identifiability and accountability so heralded in theory may in practice advantage organized groups over the public at large.

The vulnerability thesis is, however, the first to specify identifiability and accountability as the *necessary* conditions that underpin politicians' vulnerability to the demands of small groups that seek to subvert public goods. The theory is also the first to suggest that small parties are able to produce public goods because their *in*vulnerability allows them to impose concentrated costs on powerful groups—even groups within their own constituencies. Consequently, the theory requires a new model interest group influence as a product of institutional designs that foster accountability and identifiability.

Modeling Political Vulnerability

As indicated in the previous chapter, three political institutions dominate our understanding of comparative government. It is useful to think of these as "primary" institutions because each is a necessary component of any political system and fundamental to the adoption and function of other institutions.[15] All democratic political systems must define 1) how political representatives are elected, 2) how the executive is constituted, i.e., whether the regime is presidential, semi-presidential, or parliamentary, and 3) whether political power will be shared between national and subnational political actors, as in federal systems, or vested in the national government alone, as in unitary systems.

Primary institutions cannot depict every political system in all of its complexity, yet they do allow us to subsume a substantial amount of political information relevant to political vulnerability because they affect a wide range of secondary institutions. Electoral systems, for example, affect the number of parties in the party system and therein the number of parties in parliamentary executives. And, according to Strøm, the number of parties in parliamentary executives is related to the distribution of power among government and nongovernment parties in the legislature.[16] Executive regimes also have far-reaching effects, especially important to interest group strategies. Parliamentary and presidential regimes differ not just in formal executive authority, but in the origin of policy proposals and the nature of the bureaucracy.[17] And cross-national differences in state structure are strongly associated with the number of chambers in the legislature, the authority of the courts, and the independence of central banks.[18] Given that a general model must be as parsimonious as possible, model development will focus on primary institutions only.

Elections and Accountability

Political accountability ultimately requires that voters are able to remove politicians from power at the polls. Accountability is therefore located squarely in the electoral system. Given the narrow focus of this definition, it is useful to think about electoral systems as belonging to one of four groups; 1) those that return a single member from each district, 2) those that return multiple representatives per district but allow voters to remove individual politicians, 3) those that return multiple representatives per district in proportion to voter support for parties alone, and 4) those that return some representatives from SMDs and others in proportion to party support in mixed-member districts. The dynamics of each are explored below.

SINGLE-MEMBER DISTRICT SYSTEMS While electoral formulas differ, all single-member district (SMD) electoral systems return only one representative per district. Accountability is therefore immediate and direct; voters can remove their representatives in any election because only the candidate with the most votes wins the seat—all other candidates lose. Single-member district plurality (SMDP) systems, like those used in the United States and Britain, award representation to whichever candidate receives the most votes, even if the winning candidate receives less than a majority of votes. "Majority-plurality" systems like those used in France require that candidates receive a majority of votes cast on the first ballot to win the seat, or continue to a second round where a plurality will suffice but competition is limited to top vote-getters. Alternative vote systems (AV) like that used in the Australian House of Representatives allow voters to rank candidates, systematically eliminating candidates with the fewest votes until a majority winner is determined. Regardless of the specific electoral formula, the political fortunes of individual candidates hang in the balance in every election that returns a single representative per district. Voters can therefore readily remove individual politicians from power if they choose. This is of course equally true of presidential contests, as these are by definition SMD elections.[19]

SMD competition also facilitates *party* accountability to voters. Whether voters are electing a president or members of a legislature, SMD competition tends to focus voters' attention on the top two candidates in each race, only one of which will win the seat.[20] Voters' ability to remove the party that controls the executive is obvious in the case of presidential elections where the representative of only one party can claim the office. Voters hold the majority legislative party accountable separately from the executive in presidential systems, but SMD competition for legislative seats facilitates accountability of the majority party. The reason is that presidentialism tends to reduce the number of national parties to two so each can run a competitive candidate for the presidency. This fosters a two-party system at the national (as well as district) level, which allows voters to vote the majority legislative party out of power more easily.

SMD competition helps voters hold the executive accountable in parliamentary regimes as well. The translation of votes into seats in SMD systems tends to "manufacture majorities," allowing a party that wins a plurality of votes to hold a majority of legislative seats and therein govern alone.[21] Where the distribution of political preferences does not create a single majority party, two parties still tend to dominate politics and alternate in power as a single-party minority government or in coalition with a smaller party.

MULTI-MEMBER ELECTORAL SYSTEMS   Unlike SMD systems, accountability in multi-member districts (MMD) varies with electoral rules. Most multi-member electoral systems use some method of party-list proportional representation (PR) to elect individual candidates. In party-list PR systems voters are presented with competing slates of candidates prepared by each party, voters choose which party list they prefer, and when the votes are counted parties win seats in proportion to the popular support for each party (normally after meeting a minimum threshold of support and then only to the extent mathematically possible given the number of representatives returned per district). In the "closed-list" variety of PR voters cannot choose which of the party's candidates are returned because individual candidates "win" seats beginning from the top of the party-ordered list. Direct accountability to voters is low under closed-list PR because party leaders decide the order of individual candidates on party lists and are therefore more decisive than voters in determining the fate of individual politicians. Because political parties control the rank order of candidates they can also place party leaders in safe seats. As a result, it is nearly impossible for voters to remove the most influential people in the party, the people who shape party platforms, participate in government, and ultimately influence policy choice. It is the dominance of party leaders and the lack of direct accountability to voters that are the primary criticisms leveled against PR electoral systems.

"Flexible" and "open-list" PR systems allow additional voter choice through either a preference vote for a particular candidate on a party list, or a ranking of multiple candidates. Where preference votes or candidate ranking allows voters to affect outcomes, open and flexible lists enhance accountability. Where voter choice is not considered significant to outcomes, however, it remains difficult for voters to remove individual politicians from power. Accountability varies therefore with the flexibility of the list, but is as a practical matter comparatively low.

PR of any stripe makes it difficult for voters to remove political parties from power as well, especially in parliamentary systems. In PR systems voters tend to support multiple political parties, and it is rare that any individual party wins enough seats in the legislature to govern alone. The absence of a single-party majority, in government or in legislatures, necessitates multi-party coalitions to pass legislation.[22] When parties must cooperate to make policy they generally look to like-minded parties for coalition partners, relatively independent of the absolute size of their parliamentary support. As a result, parties can and do participate in parliamentary executives even when they lose vote share. This fact significantly limits accountability because even when voters withhold their support they can rarely "remove" a party from power.

While less common, some MMD systems allow voters to select among individual candidates without the aid of a party list. Nonlist electoral formulas that return multiple representatives from a single district include the single transferable vote (STV) (in Ireland and the Australian Senate) and single non-transferable vote systems (SNTV) (most notably in Japan from 1958 to 1993 and in Colombia until 2002).[23] In these systems, multiple representatives are returned from each district but candidates may run as individual party representatives, each seeking a "personal" vote. As a result, multiple representatives from the same party campaign for seats, running against members of their own party. Theoretically, voters who want to support a particular party need not support a particular candidate because voters can choose among several candidates representing that party. Practically, however, there is, as a rule, substantially less room for choice. Nevertheless, individual accountability is somewhat higher in MMD, where voters choose between individual candidates, than it is under closed-list PR, but lower than it is under SMD rules.[24]

MIXED-MEMBER SYSTEMS Mixed-member systems (MMS), those that use a combination of SMDs and PR to seat the legislature, deserve special mention. While Germany was at one time the lone example of this type of electoral system, MMS were adopted in twenty countries in the 1990s across the globe, including new democracies like Russia; transitioning democracies like Bolivia, Mexico, and Venezuela; and long-term democracies like Italy, Japan, and New Zealand. Shugart and Wattenberg (2001) suggest that MMS may offer the "best of both worlds" in terms of efficiency and representation, and it is therefore reasonable to expect that countries that change their electoral systems in the future, from either pure SMD or pure PR, will switch to mixed-member systems.[25]

Mixed-member systems seat legislators through two different methods: some are elected in SMD elections, and some are elected in larger districts that use party-list PR. Accountability is therefore complicated. The PR portion of the race remains the same, giving voters little power to actually remove candidates or parties from power. Accountability in SMD races is, by contrast, high, but it can be compromised. As one might expect, those candidates who win seats in SMD contests keep those seats; however those who lose SMD races may or may not lose power. Cross-listing of candidates on the SMD and PR portions of the ballot simultaneously generally allows party leaders and other valuable candidates high on the party list to retain power even if they lose their individual elections in SMD districts.[26]

Party accountability is also complicated in mixed-member systems. The PR portion of the ballot normally allows small parties to gain representation and concomitantly deprives large parties of majority status in the legislature. As a product of the SMD portion of the ballot, however, larger parties tend to alternate in power. Consequently accountability varies across parties. Voters can hold large parties accountable with their SMD votes but voters may or may not be able to remove smaller parties from power. Overall, therefore, accountability is expected to be higher in mixed systems than it is under pure PR because mixed systems empower parties that depend on SMD votes for political dominance.

Accountability is, however, of little value to voters or, in this case, interest groups, if they cannot identify those responsible for policy choice. Identifiability is therefore the second necessary condition underpinning political vulnerability.

Primary Institutions, Interaction Effects, and Identifiability

Identifiability refers to voters' (and interest groups') ability to identify those responsible for policy choice.[27] As suggested above, identifiability is partly a product of the electoral system. The electoral system has a strong effect on the number of parties in the party system, and the number of parties in the party system has a strong effect on the number of parties that must cooperate to make policy. The number of parties in the party system is not, however, the only determinant of the number of actors included in policy making. The number of independent political bodies with policy-making authority will affect voters and interest groups' ability to identify those responsible for ultimate policy choice. Therefore identifiability cannot be separated from regime type, i.e., whether the executive is presidential or parliamentary, because regime type is one of the primary institutions that determines the number of independent bodies with veto authority.

PARLIAMENTARY REGIMES SMD systems facilitate identifiability in parliamentary regimes because SMD competition tends to empower two large parties, one of which is normally able to govern alone with majority support in the legislature. Where single-party governments control the agenda and a parliamentary majority, policy-making responsibility is crystal clear; it belongs wholly to the party in charge.

In parliamentary regimes where the electoral rules support a multi-party system, control of the executive is normally shared among multiple political parties. Absent preelection agreements, coalition formation is generally the purview of the party winning the most votes, and the leader of the largest party conventionally invites one or more smaller parties close on the ideological spectrum to share executive power. Given the need for parliamentary majorities to pass legislation, the number of seats controlled by these smaller parties is important, but not all important. The like-mindedness of a party on matters high on the political agenda is likely to be more important in terms of coalition potential. Sometimes the largest party cannot find coalition partners and the second largest party attempts to form a government instead. Sometimes no majority coalition is possible and a minority party governs with support from legislative parties on either a regular or an ad hoc basis. Regardless of how or where coalitions are formed, however, ultimately identifiability for policy choices is obscured by the need to cooperate and compromise. The more parties included in the executive or, in the case of minority government, included in the legislative coalition supporting a particular policy choice, the more identifiability is obscured.[28]

PRESIDENTIAL AND SEMI-PRESIDENTIAL REGIMES Identifiability for policy choice is obscured in presidential and semi-presidential regimes, even (in the fairly rare instances) where SMD contests generate two-party systems.[29] This is clear under "divided government" because one party controls one or more houses of the legislature and the other party controls the executive. Voters are very likely to know the preferences of the parties controlling different branches of government, but where parties must compromise to make policy it is difficult to blame one party for negotiated outcomes. Importantly, some scholars argue that compromise is often required under unified government as well, i.e., even when the same party controls the legislature and the executive.[30] The argument is based on the assumption that politicians' policy preferences reflect those of their constituents. Given that the president is elected by the national electorate and individual legislators represent much smaller constituencies, it is reasonable to expect political disagreements even among representatives of the same political party. The American experience with unified government certainly supports the claim.

The identifiability of policy makers in multi-party presidential systems is, however, a much more difficult question. The problem is that presidents are highly identifiable and usually very powerful. While one may reasonably expect policy making to be less identifiable where multiple parties must form legislative coalitions, if legislative coalitions fail to come to agreement presidents can often step into the vacuum and make policy by decree. Even without decrees, presidents are inclined to initiate major changes from above, creating policy *faits accomplis* for parties that have little choice but to go along with the president as the leader of the party.[31] Where this is the case, identifiability for policy choice may be higher than it is in presidential regimes that use SMD elections for the legislature. Regardless of the number of parties in the party system, however, identifiability for policy choice is obscured in presidential and semi-presidential systems by the need for compromise among independent political bodies.[32]

HOW FEDERALISM MATTERS: POLICY POSITIONS VS. POLICY CHOICE

The division of power between national and subnational governments does not directly affect accountability because it does not affect the ability of voters to remove politicians from power. Identifiability is another issue, however, and a complicated one. It is reasonable to expect that federalism will obscure identifiability for ultimate policy choice if the popularly elected assembly is required to share power with an independent political body that represents constituent states. Paradoxically, however, federalism also enhances the identifiability of representatives who are explicitly responsible for advancing and protecting subnational interests. The paradox derives from the unique nature of their mandate.

Representatives in the second chamber must take policy positions on issues most important to their constituents. Their votes on issues disproportionately salient to local interests are normally well publicized, and they campaign based on their ability to advance and protect subnational interests at the national level. As a result, representatives of subnational constituencies are arguably more accountable for whether or not their choices reflect subnational preferences than they are for the ultimate policy choice. In other words, voters—and interest groups—need only link their state representatives to their individual votes affecting the state to assess performance, not ultimate policy outcomes. Consequently, politicians who represent subnational interests in a second chamber are highly identifiable. If those representatives are also highly accountable, they are likely to be vulnerable to interest group demands. If the electoral system does not allow voters to hold those representatives accountable, however, identifiability will not have as great an impact on vulnerability.

Expectations: Variance in Vulnerability with Institutional Design

The assessment of primary institutions in terms of identifiability and accountability suggests a number of specific expectations regarding institutional design. Identifiability and accountability are maximized in parliamentary systems where politicians are elected by SMD; both are minimized in parliamentary systems where politicians are elected by party-list PR. Presidential systems fall somewhere between these extremes. Federalism has no independent effect on accountability but does enhance the identifiability of politicians elected to represent the interests of constituent states at the national level. Table 2.1 summarizes expectations regarding the institutionalized vulnerability associated with primary institutions.

These expectations differ from the veto-based models discussed in the previous chapter. Recall that veto-based models associate interest group influence with minority representation and therein the multiplicity of veto players inherent in political systems that divide power among multiple political parties or multiple political bodies. Those who associate interest group advantages with weak executive authority or low levels of party discipline anticipate that parliamentary systems will outperform their presidential counterparts. The vulnerability-based model, by contrast, links interest group influence to institutions that concentrate political power in one political party.

System-level expectations of the vulnerability thesis are also clearly at odds with conventional veto-based models. Veto-based models anticipate that parliamentary regimes will be less vulnerable to interest group influence than presidential regimes, and that unitary systems will be less vulnerable than federal systems. By contrast, the vulnerability thesis locates the greatest source of interest group influence in the electoral system, posits interactive effects for regime type, and anticipates mixed but predictable effects resulting from state structure. Table 2.2 compares expectations regarding individual institutions.

Table 2.1. Vulnerability thesis—expectations for interest group influence

	Lowest	Moderate	Highest
Electoral system	Closed party-list PR	Accountable MMD	SMD
	Flexible-list PR	(STV/SNTV)	
	Open-list PR		
	MMS		
Executive regime	Parliamentary/PR	Presidential	Parliamentary/SMD
Division of power	Unitary		Federal

Table 2.2. Minority representation; party discipline and vulnerability

Causal mechanism	Least vulnerable	→	→	→	Most vulnerable
Minority representation/ veto players	SMD parliamentary unitary				PR presidential federal
Party discipline*	SMD parliamentary	PR parliamentary	PR presidential	SMD presidential	
Vulnerability (to interest group demands)	PR parliamentary unitary	PR presidential	SMD presidential	SMD parliamentary federal	

*Gerring and Thacker (2008) argue that PR/parliamentary systems can impose stronger party discipline than SMD/parliamentary systems because parties determine the rank ordering of candidates on party lists. Placement here reflect arguments that party discipline is stronger in SMD/parliamentary systems because defections by the rank and file are less important to a party's power in PR systems than they are in SMD systems, i.e., because the costs of defection are higher in two-party systems the likelihood of defection is lower. Note, however, that the relative placement of the two systems is not critical, as expectations remain different from models reflecting other causal mechanisms regardless of placement of the two systems.

COMPARING DEMOCRACIES: A HIERARCHICAL MODEL As indicated above, many scholars argue that comparative models of democracies must be organized around institutional combinations, not individual institutions.[33] Contrary to other models, however, the vulnerability thesis gives theoretical prominence to the role of the electoral system, suggesting that we can rank the contribution of individual institutions to system vulnerability hierarchically.

The electoral system has the most significant effect because it has a nearly deterministic effect on both accountability and identifiability. SMD systems are essential to accountability; PR systems essentially preclude accountability. Therefore, the first question that should organize our understanding of political institutions pertains to the electoral system: Are representatives returned via PR, a mixed or highly accountable multiple-member system, or SMD? The impact of executive regime is secondary, as the accountability and identifiability of presidential and parliamentary regimes will differ depending on whether the electoral system generates partisan power that is unified, divided, or fragmented among multiple

Table 2.3. The vulnerability continuum

Least interest group power		→	→	→		Most interest group power					
PR			Non-PR			SMD					
(Closed/Flexible/Open)			multi-member								
MMS			(STV/SNTV)								
Parliamentary		Presidential		Parliamentary		Presidential		Presidential		Parliamentary	
U	F	U	F	U	F	U	F	U	F	U	F

political parties.[34] State structure is a tertiary concern, as its impact has no direct effect on accountability.

Table 2.3 indicates placement of political systems on a continuum based on politicians' predicted vulnerability to interest group influence. Individual systems are defined by three primary institutions: the electoral system, the regime type, and state organization. Given that the vulnerability resulting from electoral formula is more important than regime type or state organization, differences in electoral formula divide political systems into two large groups; those using party-list PR and those that use SMDs, with STV and SNTV, the two MMD systems that allow voters to choose among candidates, between the two. A second distinction is made with regard to regime type; presidential systems fall in the middle of the continuum, parliamentary systems at either end. The federal-unitary distinction determines the third distinction, with unitary systems being associated with less identifiability than federal systems.

The comparative model is now ready for testing. Note that it offers stark contrasts between the thesis and conventional theories.[35] Veto-based arguments that link minority representation and party discipline to interest group influence anticipate that the SMD/parliamentary/unitary combination will generate the least vulnerability to interest group demands. Yet the vulnerability-based model anticipates that these governments will be among the most vulnerable, and therefore the least able to provide the public good when the costs must fall on organized groups. The proof is, as they say, in the pudding. The next chapter identifies an appropriate case to test the model and develops a vulnerability-based index to allow quantitative analyses of cross-national differences in policy choice.

3

EVIDENCE FROM THE ENVIRONMENT

The previous chapter introduced a general theory of interest group influence in democratic countries. The vulnerability thesis anticipates that the structure of political institutions will generate cross-national differences in the vulnerability of policy makers to interest group demands, and therein governments' ability to provide public goods that impose concentrated costs on organized groups. This chapter identifies the conditions necessary to test the model and begins to explore the evidence for anticipated differences.

The investigation proceeds in two steps. The first section identifies countries suitable for comparative analysis and an appropriate test case for study. Case selection is essential to research design because political institutions and key alternative explanations for policy choice co-vary, making it difficult to identify cases that offer a definitive test of the institutional determinants of interest group influence on policy. After careful consideration, however, we find that policies designed to reduce farmers' use of agrochemicals provide an excellent vehicle to test the theory.

The second section tests the thesis, beginning with an examination of the relationship between institutional design and policy choices in that policy area. We find dramatic cross-national differences in policy choice consistent with the vulnerability thesis. Decades of data on agrochemical use motivate the development of a "Vulnerability Index" to allow quantitative analyses of the impact of institutions on agrochemical use relative to alternative explanations. The section concludes with a report of the results and a summary discussion of the relationship between institutional design and cross-national changes in agrochemical use.

Country and Case Selection

Given the number of important factors that can affect policy choice, the countries chosen for this initial test must meet three criteria. First, the countries selected must be long-standing democracies of varying institutional designs capable of demonstrating clear institutional effects on policy choice. Second, their economies must be strong enough to allow government imposition of costs on economic groups. Third, the countries included must be capable of choosing similar policy instruments.

Country Selection and Time Period Studied

The twenty countries that have been continuously democratic since approximately the end of World War II—Australia, Austria, Belgium, Canada, Denmark, Finland, France, West Germany, Iceland, Ireland, Italy, Japan, Luxembourg, the Netherlands, New Zealand, Norway, Sweden, Switzerland, the United Kingdom, and the United States— constitute the largest set of countries that unquestionably meet all three criteria. Most institutional scholars are also well acquainted with these systems, and a substantial body of research already links institutions in these countries to policy choices that may reflect government capacity to impose costs or provide public goods. Consequently, this set of countries offers the additional benefit of allowing other scholars to assess the efficacy of the vulnerability thesis relative to alternative explanations reviewed in the previous chapter based on personal knowledge of the states.

Table 3.1 locates each of these countries on the vulnerability continuum developed in the previous chapter based on the design of individual political systems. Given that theoretical placement is defined by primary institutions, the location of most countries is straightforward. The far left side of the table includes countries characterized by the set of institutions argued to leave policy makers least vulnerable to interest group demands, i.e., the parliamentary and unitary states that use closed-list proportional representation (PR). The far right side includes all single-member district

Table 3.1. The vulnerability continuum (applied)

Least vulnerable to interest groups → → →							*Most vulnerable to interest groups*	
PR/MMS				MMD	SMD			
Parliamentary		Presidential			Presidential		Parliamentary	
Unitary	Federal	Unitary	Federal	U/F	Unitary	Federal	Unitary	Federal
BEL	AUT			IRE		USA	FRA*	AUS
DNK	DEU*			JPN			NZL	CAN
FIN*	CHE						GBR	
ISL								
ITA*								
LUX								
NLD								
NOR								
SWE								

* Finland, France, Germany, and Italy shift location due to deviations from ideal type; see text for description.

(SMD) countries that are parliamentary and federal. Other institutional designs locate countries between the two extremes.

The positions of four countries are adjusted to reflect the extent of accountability and identifiability generated by variance in key attributes of individual institutions, especially those of the electoral system. Germany's position shifts because mixed-member electoral systems increase accountability for those members of legislature elected in SMDs and enhance the identifiability of governments dominated by large parties that normally alternate in government.[1] The positions of Finland and Italy shift to reflect the greater accountability of open-list PR, which allows citizens to vote for specific candidates within party lists. Regime-type differences are limited to France, where one could argue that the reduced identifiability of France's semi-presidential system more properly locates it between the United Kingdom and the United States.

The conventional use of long-standing democracies is predicated on the assumption that institutions are stable in these countries, and therefore policy choices reflect institutionalized incentives. While this was long a safe assumption, changes to primary institutions in the early-to-mid 1990s in Belgium, Japan, Italy, and New Zealand complicate comparison after 1995.

Consequently, comparison without modification for institutional change is appropriate only for the period from 1950, when democratic institutions were imposed in Germany and Japan, until 1995, when those identified above changed primary institutions.

Case Selection: Ideology and Corporatism as the Critical Considerations

Given the frequency with which pundits and politicians point to interest group gains at public expense, one might reasonably expect that a plethora of cases would be available to test the theory. As discussed in the introduction however, this is not the case. The first challenge is to identify public goods that are neutral ideologically. Ideological neutrality is a critical consideration because competing conceptualizations of the public interest are often grounded in the proper role of the state in the economy. Where voters elect parties of the right, for example, the public has arguably decided that minimal government intervention in the economy, i.e., low taxes and few restrictions on economic activity, is in its best interest. Where voters elect parties of the left, the public has arguably decided that government actions designed to reduce inequalities, i.e., progressive tax rates or redistributive welfare state policies that benefit disadvantaged groups, are in its best interest.[2] This suggests that the comparative analysis of some policies will not offer a clear test of the model absent controls for the ideological predispositions of governments that could explain cross-national variance.

The need for this control presents a significant challenge to research design. Research shows that states that use PR are generally governed by parties of the left (seventy-five percent of non-center governments), while political systems that use SMD elections are governed by parties of the right by about the same margin.[3] As a result, the electoral system, the institution argued to be at the source of politicians' vulnerability to interest group demands, is strongly correlated with the ideological complexion of government, which is an alternative explanation for policy choice. Moreover, the inertia of policy legacies suggests that we may not be able to control for modal government ideology by measuring the ideology of individual governments. It would, for example, be unreasonable to expect intermittent governing coalitions of conservative parties to undo decades of Social Democratic dominance in Sweden.

Cross-national variance in the system of interest group representation presents a similar problem; countries that use PR tend to be corporatist, countries that use SMD tend to be pluralist. In corporatist systems, most organized groups that represent business and labor belong to hierarchically structured peak organizations that allow their highest representatives to negotiate policy in cooperation with the state. As a result, corporatist systems are characterized by relatively few interest groups, each of which encompasses a broad segment of the citizenry. Pluralist systems, by contrast, do not regulate the participation of interest groups, nor do they delegate formal policy-making power to interest groups. Consequently, pluralist systems are characterized by a multitude of relatively small groups.

Cross-national differences in the system of interest group representation is an important factor affecting policy choice because we expect that large groups will prefer policies that provide broad benefits, while small groups will prefer policies with targeted benefits.[4] Moreover, the strong empirical correlation between the electoral system and interest group system suggests that a causal relationship may exist between the party system and the system of interest group representation. The links between PR, corporatism, and welfare state policies are especially clear. PR has long been associated with the empowerment of labor because it allows political parties with narrow ideological appeals to gain power. Labor unions have historically mobilized to support "labor" parties, and their numbers often propel them into government. In return, labor parties support institutionalized corporatist arrangements that require business to negotiate with labor over wages and benefits. Corporatist decision making also includes the state in tripartite negotiations, which has resulted in state-sponsored health care, housing, and job training programs that reduce inequality in many countries. Mutual benefits perpetuate these relationships and labor's influence on policy choice. As a result, it is difficult to assess the independent role of political institutions on cross-national differences in policies associated with the welfare state, especially those that decommodify labor by providing universal benefits as a right of citizenship.

EVIDENCE FROM THE ENVIRONMENT: CASE-BASED CONSIDERATIONS

Given these concerns, environmental policies are arguably the most comparable measures of governments' ability to impose concentrated costs to provide public goods. Unlike ideological differences regarding the role of private and public suppliers of health care, there are no private providers of environmental services. This is not to say that there are no disputes over the proper amount of environmental regulation, yet few condone uncompensated externalities that threaten or diminish the capacity of the public commons to support life or economic development.

That said, not all environmental policies offer a valid test of the thesis. Two considerations stand out. First, environmental protection that requires governments to impose diffuse costs, as in the development of water treatment facilities or recycling programs, does not offer a valid test of interest group influence.[5] Second, case selection must control for critical cross-national differences in resource endowments that present significant obstacles to assessing the independent role of institutions in pollution abatement. Geographical differences in energy supplies are, for example, often the source of cross-national differences in the structure of the manufacturing sector, the relative cost of polluting activities, and ultimately the pollutants generated.[6] Therefore, where coal is cheap and plentiful we expect a country's industrial and energy sectors to be fueled by it; where coal is scarce other fuels are likely to be more important to economic development. Consequently, cross-national differences in commonly measured pollutants like carbon dioxide, nitrous oxides, and sulfur dioxide emissions are likely to reflect natural resource endowments in energy supplies, making it almost impossible to fully control for differences between states.

The Test Case: Agrochemical Pollution Therefore, few environmental policy areas present a better opportunity to conduct a decisive test of the theory than those that affect the use of chemicals in agriculture. Unlike many other environmental issues, cross-national differences in resource endowments and economic structure are trivial. Consequently policies targeted at agrochemical use allow us to assess the role of institutions in environmental performance more reliably than in many other environmental measures.

Policies that affect agriculture also present a rare opportunity to control for the theoretical impacts of corporatism. Agriculture is one of the few policy areas where differences between pluralist and corporatist democracies are relatively inconsequential. While small in membership, agricultural groups in both pluralist and corporatist systems are well organized and politically powerful beyond their numbers. In both types of interest group systems agriculture has insider status, with a demonstrated and well recognized ability to shape much of the legislation that governs the agriculture industry in general.[7] In addition, unlike the competitive and "countervailing" relationship between labor and management groups during wage and income policy making, agricultural organizations do not face structured opposition in corporatist systems.[8] As a result, the size of agricultural interest groups, their influence on policy choice, and the extent to which they face structured opposition, i.e., the three attributes that differentiate interest group demands in pluralist and corporatist systems, are in this policy area equal.

Abatement of agrochemical pollution also clearly pits the provision of public goods against interest group preferences; requiring policy makers to impose concentrated costs on farmers and agrochemical manufacturers (some of the most powerful groups in domestic politics) to achieve environmental goals. Policy makers are well aware that pesticides and fertilizers are important agricultural inputs for farmers, one of the very few controls farmers enjoy over the vagaries of climate and pests, with immediate impacts on the quantity and quality of food that farmers can produce. For agrochemical manufacturers, products are extremely expensive to develop, and they require relatively long market lives to provide adequate returns on the investment.

Policy makers are also aware that the imprudent use of fertilizers and pesticides poses serious long-term threats to public health and the natural environment, and that the environmental problems associated with agrochemicals are largely due to waste.[9] The method by which most agrochemicals are usually applied, i.e., machine spraying, generates significant losses from evaporation and negatively affects many nontarget species, including birds and farm animals. Once on the land, agrochemicals often wash into surface and groundwater with rain and irrigation. Even under the most judicious application methods, however, agrochemicals that enter the environment to increase crop production in one season often remain as contaminates for years after their usefulness.

One of the most significant threats results from the use of nitrogen fertil-izers. Surplus nitrogen loading to both surface and groundwater is widely considered the most serious agriculture-based pollutant. Heavy nitrogen loading causes eutrophication, a process wherein increased nitrogen spurs algae growth, which in turn exhausts most of the available oxygen in the water, leaving inadequate amounts for fish and other organisms. Large-scale eutrophication like that in the Gulf of Mexico, where runoff from U.S. farms creates an annual "dead zone" the size of New Jersey, is responsible for fish kills around the world.[10] Nitrous oxide, which is produced as a by-product when nitrogen is broken down in the soil, is also a greenhouse gas, hundreds of times more potent than carbon dioxide, and agriculture is its major source.[11] And in regions without clean drinking water, high levels of nitrate contamination reduce the blood's capacity to transport oxygen, resulting in "blue baby syndrome."[12]

Pesticides pose potentially more serious but less obvious problems. Nontarget species not poisoned with an initial direct pesticide contact may be unable to reproduce; and the elimination of a target pest can affect the food chain, having delayed affects on nontarget species that rely on agricultural pests for food.[13] Because pesticides bioaccumulate and magnify as they pass through the food chain, they pose special threats to human populations. Exposure to pesticides through contact or ingestion has been linked to an increased risk of thyroid cancer, cancers of reproductive organs, reduced sperm counts, infertility, weakened immune systems, Parkinson's disease, and attention-deficit/hyperactivity disorder (ADHD).[14]

Given the severe environmental consequences of agrochemical pollution, it is reasonable to expect that agrochemical use would be limited to that necessary to protect crops and maximize yields. Yet research at the farm level indicates that this is not the case. In Norway, for example, Veldeld (1998) found that the large variation of nitrogen use on farms could not be explained by agricultural requisites. Usage levels also cannot be explained by economics; Nieuwenhuize et al. (1995) showed that 41 percent of Dutch dairy farmers could actually improve their profits by an average of 13 percent by lowering nitrogen use.[15] In fact, extension service research conducted in Sweden demonstrates that the use of some agrochemicals can be decreased by up to 50 percent without affecting yields.[16] Therefore, cross-national differences in agrochemical use present us with an empirically interesting puzzle.

One of the most likely explanations is that, despite the economic inefficiencies of overuse and the serious environmental and health problems associated with agrochemicals, regulation in this area is not easy. The political problems associated with regulating agrochemicals are similar to those inherent in regulating most environmental threats; long and complex time lags between cause and effect generate uncertainty and increase the extent to which policy makers and the public alike discount risks. Therefore, the question is, do cross-national differences in political vulnerability have a measurable effect on governments' ability to impose concentrated costs on farmers and agrochemical manufacturers to protect the public good?

Measuring Vulnerability: Cross-National Differences in Policy Choice

A finite number of policy instruments are available to policy makers in developed countries who want to address the environmental problems associated with agrochemicals. Governments can choose to tax agrochemicals, regulate the availability of chemicals via registration requirements, impose education requirements on farmers to reduce the likelihood of misuse, or demand that farm machinery be tested and certified to eliminate waste. Taxes are the most efficient instrument because they allow governments to target costs very precisely on specific agrochemicals. Because taxes impose immediate and concentrated costs, they are also a good measure of government capacity to overcome interest group resistance to policy change. Stringent registration requirements are also an effective measure, potentially allowing governments to ban the most dangerous products and requiring chemical manufacturers to conduct exhaustive tests before new products are introduced to the market. Farmer education requirements and certification requirements for farm machinery target farmers directly in an effort to reduce waste and improper use at the farm level.

The vulnerability thesis posits linkages between institutions and policy choice and between policy choice and the provision of public goods. Therefore the first place to look for evidence of interest group power is in policy choice. We should find the use of policy instruments described above more common in political systems that leave policy makers least vulnerable to interest group demands, and least common in political systems where politicians are accountable and identifiable. Table 3.2 summarizes the findings of an extensive review and assessment of policies conducted by the OECD in 1996, and supplementary policy information collected by the United Nations in 1992. If either of these international organizations reported the use of policy instruments in any of these areas the corresponding cell is marked "yes." For ease of analysis, countries are listed in order of their placement on the vulnerability continuum above.

Table 3.2. Policies targeting agrochemical use (1970–1995)

	Taxes	Stringent chemical regulations	Stringent education requirements	Stringent certification requirements
Belgium and Luxembourg*	—	—	—	—
Denmark	Yes	Yes	Yes	Yes
Iceland	—	—	—	—
Netherlands	—	—	Yes	—
Norway	Yes	Yes	—	Yes
Sweden	Yes	Yes	Yes	Yes
Austria	Yes	Yes	Yes	—
Finland	Yes	—	—	Yes
Italy	—	—	—	—
Switzerland	—	—	—	—
Germany	—	Yes	Yes	Yes
Ireland	—	—	—	—
Japan	—	—	—	—
United States	—	—	—	—
France	—	—	—	—
New Zealand	—	—	—	—
United Kingdom	—	—	—	—
Australia	—	—	—	—
Canada	—	—	—	—

* Belgium and Luxembourg are treated as one country because they report their agricultural statistics together and cannot be separated. As both countries are parliamentary and unitary, and use a PR electoral system, their treatment as a single country poses no theoretical problems.

Consistent with theoretical expectations, there are significant cross-national differences in policy choice. Policy makers in countries that use PR of any stripe, unitary and federal, have utilized a variety of instruments to achieve environmental goals. By contrast, policy makers elected in SMDs and highly accountable multi-member districts (MMDs) have not used any of the instruments available to them to affect a reduction in use. The evidence could not be clearer. While there is some variance within PR countries, the significant difference is between PR and non-PR countries.

Institutional analyses are often forced to stop at this point, as it is generally difficult to move beyond policy choice to measurable environmental outcomes. Fortunately this is not the case here; the use of agricultural inputs in advanced democracies has been measured reliably for decades. Consequently we have extensive data on the aggregate use of fertilizers and pesticides in developed countries and changes in their use over time. Moreover, agrochemical use demonstrably equates with environmental impact so it is reasonable to expect that changes in use have environmental consequences.[17] As a result, we have the opportunity to ask the next logical question, i.e., do cross-national differences in governments' imposition of concentrated costs affect the provision of public goods?

The Vulnerability Index

Given the availability of data, we need a way to quantify differences in political institutions to allow quantitative analysis. The hierarchical model developed in the previous chapter anticipates a clear hierarchical ranking of political systems based on institutional configurations. The continuum does not, however, allow us to use these rankings in a quantitative analysis because it does not posit specific distances between political systems. The theoretical interdependence of electoral system, regime type, and state organization, and the small number of countries studied, argue against the use of categorical variables to estimate relative positions. The model does, however, lend itself to the creation of an interval index that ranks political systems relative to one another based on the theoretical expectations regarding the relative importance of primary institutions.

To capture the relative importance of primary institutions, the simplest interval range assigns one point to state organization, two points to regime type and three to the electoral system. The exact numerical difference between political systems may not be perfect, but these values accurately reflect the posited *relative* affect of primary institutions. The theory posits that the electoral system will have the greatest impact on vulnerability, affecting accountability via elections and identifiability of governments. Regime type is of secondary importance because cross-national differences between presidential and parliamentary regimes affect identifiability but not accountability. Differences between unitary and federal systems have the least influence on country placement because they have no effect on accountability and mixed effects on identifiability.

To allow for adequate relative differentiation of primary institutions among PR systems, the valuation requires that PR systems as a group constitute four intervals at one end of the continuum: one for PR systems that are parliamentary and unitary, a second for PR systems that are parliamentary and federal, a third for PR systems that are presidential and unitary, and a fourth for PR systems that are presidential and federal. SMD systems will necessarily constitute four points at the other end. Given the theoretical importance of highly accountable MMD systems, at least one interval should be reserved for these systems.[18] Other than country-specific shifts due to electoral formula, i.e., closed- vs. open-list PR, no other point differences are theoretically justified. Thus, Table 3.3 indicates the placement most faithful to a minimalist interpretation of the theoretical model.

On the far left, with an index rating of "o," are parliamentary and unitary systems that use closed-list PR. These countries are assigned a rating of "o" because this set of institutions minimizes vulnerability to the greatest extent possible; no other combination of primary institutions can further limit the ability of interest groups to punish politicians for legislation that imposes concentrated costs on small but powerful groups. As discussed above,

Table 3.3. The vulnerability index*

PR				*MMD*			*SMD*	
Parliamentary		Presidential			Presidential		Parliamentary	
U	F	U	F	U/F	U	F	U	F
o	I	2	3	4	5	6	7	8

* From least vulnerable to interest group influence to most vulnerable.

however, it is necessary to adjust country placement to reflect differences in electoral rules. Therefore the more accountable open-list PR systems shift one index point as do mixed-member systems that use SMD and PR elections. Systems that are PR/parliamentary but also federal are assigned a value of "1" on the scale. Political systems that combine party-list PR with presidentialism in a unitary state are assigned a value of "2." There are no countries that use presidential systems in federal states that use PR in this study, but if there were they would be assigned a ranking of "3" to reflect the increased vulnerability associated with presidentialism and federalism.

Countries that use SMD elections are in the latter half of the index, ranging across four index points to allow valuations equal to those of PR systems above. If presidential and unitary, SMD countries would be assigned a value of "5"; if presidential and federal a "6." Parliamentary systems that use SMD are assigned a "7" if unitary and an "8" if federal. Non-PR, multiple-member districts constitute a middle interval, assigned a value of "4" to reflect the theoretical distinctiveness of these systems.

No doubt scholars will disagree on the exact placement of individual countries; however, the assignments capture the relative role of primary institutions without going beyond the theoretical relationships posited. It is therefore a very good place to start. Table 3.4 indicates the location of individual countries on the vulnerability index.

The first interval includes the seven PR countries that are both parliamentary and unitary, i.e., Belgium, Denmark, Iceland, Luxembourg, the Netherlands, Norway, and Sweden. The federal states—i.e., Austria, Germany, and Switzerland—are assigned to the second interval with a ranking of "1." As stated above, electoral-system-generated increases in accountability affect the placement of Germany, Finland, and Italy, with each country moving one point on the index.[19]

A single interval between PR and SMD systems is reserved for electoral systems wherein politicians run as individuals in MMDs that do not distribute seats in proportion to the first votes of voters. Ireland's use of the single transferable vote (STV) and Japan's use of the single non-transferable vote (SNTV) locates each of these two countries in this category. This distinction is consistent with the institutional literature; scholars generally create a separate category for "semi-proportional" systems to recognize the substantial differences between these systems and those that use PR or SMD.

Table 3.4: The vulnerability index—country location

| PR | | | | MMD | SMD | | | |
| Parliamentary | | Presidential | | | Presidential | | Parliamentary | |
U	F	U	F	U/F	U	F	U	F
0	1	2	3	4	5	6	7	8
BEL	AUT			IRE		USA	FRA*	AUS
DNK	DEU*			JPN			NZL	CAN
FIN*	CHE						GBR	
ISL								
ITA*								
LUX								
NLD								
NOR								
SWE								

* Finland, France, Germany, and Italy shift location due to deviations from ideal type; see text for description.

Placement among the SMD systems follows the same rules as placement in the PR systems. Note, however, that the theory predicts that presidential systems will be less vulnerable than parliamentary systems when combined with SMD elections. If presidential and unitary, SMD countries would be assigned a value of "5"; if presidential and federal (the United States) a "6." Parliamentary systems that use SMD are assigned a "7" if unitary (Britain) and an "8" if federal (Australia and Canada).[20] To reflect France's semi-presidential executive regime, its location shifts to "6.5," between Britain and the United States.

Cross-National Differences in Agrochemical Use

To gauge the relative changes in pollution from agrochemicals we must look at historical *trends* in the usage of fertilizers and pesticides rather than at cross-national differences in absolute usage. While absolute usage demonstrably equates with environmental harm, and reductions in use can therefore be equated with environmental benefits, comparative analysis of absolute usage levels is inappropriate for two reasons. First, crop, climate, and soil requisites vary significantly with geography, affecting which inputs a farmer will use and at what level. Second, absolute usage is not a valid measure of interest group influence; it does not reflect government ability to resist interest group demands or impose concentrated costs. The task at hand is to assess whether or not the advanced democracies witnessed *changes* in agrochemical use consistent with the enactment of policies described above after they learned that agrochemicals pose dangers to human and natural systems.

Table 3.5 presents summary usage statistics for the three fertilizers used on crops, i.e., nitrogen, phosphorous, and potassium, and all types of pesticides as a group. The time period studied begins in 1970, as the simultaneous emergence of environmental awareness across the West in the late 1960s marked the initiation of modern environmental policy across industrialized states.[21] The ending date of 1995 is, as discussed above, dictated by the research design; primary institutions changed in Belgium, Italy, Japan, and New Zealand in the mid-1990s. Coincidently, the time period also allows us to control for the fact that the agri-environmental policies of Austria, Finland, and Sweden were altered by their entry to the European Union in 1995.

Countries are listed in the table in ascending order according to the index ranking, i.e., from the best able to provide public goods demanding concentrated costs to the least able to do so. The four variables measuring agrochemical use are listed in subsequent columns; they include one for each fertilizer, i.e., nitrogen, phosphorus, and potassium, and one for all pesticides as a group. The values reported are for input use per hectare of arable land and permanent crops in 1995 as a percent of the use in 1970.[22]

The bottom section of the table highlights interesting comparisons among subgroups. The most striking difference is between the eleven countries at the top of the table that use PR and the eight countries at the bottom of the table that elect representatives in SMDs or accountable MMDs. The PR countries increased their usage of nitrogen on average by approximately 10 percent over the twenty-five-year period studied. During those same years the accountable MMD and SMD systems increased their usage on average by 200 percent. Increases in nitrogen usage are especially alarming given that nitrogen fertilizers have been the target of reduction policies longer than any other input.

Table 3.5. Trends in agrochemical use in twenty countries (1970–1995)

	Institutional index	Nitrogen use per hectare	Phosphorus use per hectare	Potassium use per hectare	Pesticide use per hectare
Belgium/ Luxembourg	0	1.16	0.42	0.60	—
Denmark	0	1.11	0.42	0.62	1.15
Iceland	0	0.96	0.82	0.87	—
Netherlands	0	0.85	0.50	0.53	0.54
Norway	0	1.19	0.50	0.80	0.44
Sweden	0	1.04	0.38	0.43	0.28
Austria	1	0.99	0.52	0.42	1.14
Finland	1	1.28	0.49	0.74	0.54
Italy	1	2.14	1.46	2.58	1.23
Switzerland	1	1.41	0.58	0.50	0.94
Germany	2	1.11	0.31	0.37	1.40
Ireland	4	5.09	0.81	1.22	2.23
Japan	4	0.97	1.21	1.00	0.78
United States	6	1.61	1.00	1.33	1.28
France	6.5	1.61	0.56	1.05	1.99
New Zealand	7	5.22	1.29	1.27	—
United Kingdom	7	2.10	0.83	1.07	1.31
Australia	8	4.56	0.99	2.19	—
Canada	8	4.95	1.83	1.73	—
Group averages					
All PR countries	0–3	1.20	0.58	0.77	0.85
All SMD & MMD countries	4–8	3.26	1.07	1.36	1.51
PR & unitary	0	1.05	0.51	0.64	0.60
PR & federal	1	1.17	0.47	0.43	1.16
Accountable PR	1–2	1.71	0.98	1.66	0.89
MMDs	4	3.03	1.01	1.11	1.51
SMD/presidential	5–6	2.97	0.89	1.13	1.65
SMD/parliamentary	7–8	3.71	1.27	1.75	1.28

Trends in the use of phosphorous and potassium fertilizers are similar. While the PR countries reduced their usage of phosphorus by almost half from 1970 to 1995, farmers in SMD and accountable MMD systems either maintained their usage or increased it slightly on average. While the PR countries reduced their usage of potassium by 20 percent per hectare, the SMD and accountable MMDs increased their usage by an average of one third. The figures for usage of pesticides show a trend in the same direction, but it should be noted that sufficient data is not available for six countries: Australia, Belgium/Luxembourg, Canada, Iceland, and New Zealand. In addition, pesticide data is based on a shorter time period.[23]

Comparing subgroups allows us to identify how certain institutions associated with the same or similar electoral systems contribute to the averages of the larger groups. The unitary systems using closed-list PR have consistently shown the most significant reduction in agrochemical use. However, the federal systems that use PR are a close second in overall performance, suggesting that federalism does not have a significant effect on ultimate changes in use. Raw data for the countries classified as having open lists is mixed. Nevertheless, the electoral system is associated with trends in usage regardless of the internal distribution of power, as the theory predicts.

Correlation analysis confirms that PR systems are associated with reductions in all types of fertilizer use over time. Bivariate analyses using Ordinary Least Squares (OLS) indicate that these relationships are all statistically significant. The index is also correlated with changes in agrochemical use, and bivariate regressions show that the index demonstrates higher statistical significance than the SMD/PR distinction alone. Pesticide use, while moderately correlated with the index, does not demonstrate a statistically significant relationship with institutional structure in bivariate regressions. Raw trend data is, however, only suggestive; we must control for the effects of many other variables that impact agrochemical use before conclusions can be made.

Alternative Explanations: Identifying Control Variables

Absent the theory-driven examination of agrochemical use here, there is no reason to expect that the structure of governmental institutions will affect something as remote as farmers' choices of fertilizers and pesticides in the field. In fact, the argument on its face is the least intuitive explanation of cross-national variance in agrochemical usage trends. Undoubtedly three alternative explanations for cross-national variance in agrochemical use must be considered. The most intuitive explanation for differences across states is that changes in agricultural requisites due to crop or climate drive changes in agrochemical use. Economic factors may also affect input use. Agricultural subsidies may encourage farmers to use more inputs, and cross-national differences in the economic value of agriculture or chemical manufacturing may affect government regulation of domestic industries. Finally, public preferences for environmental goods are also likely to affect government policy. We consider each below.

AGRICULTURAL REQUISITES Comparing trends in agrochemical use rather than absolute usage levels provides a natural control for variations in climate and stable cropping patterns. To control for large changes affecting aggregate measures we must, however, control for change in cropping patterns in major crops. Changes in land area devoted to wheat, barley, potatoes, sugar beets, and oilseed rape are the crops considered here.[24] As changes in crop mix and agrochemical use are slow, the difference between the 1970 and 1995 annual value should suffice to measure trends.[25]

ECONOMIC CONSIDERATIONS The primary economic consideration for farmers is commodity price. Commodity prices are important because they affect farmers' choice regarding what to grow and therein the need for specific inputs in specific quantities. Theoretically, therefore, increases in agrochemical use associated with the production of a particular crop should be captured by the change in the land devoted to major crops variable discussed above. Nevertheless, a control for cross-national differences in subsidy levels is desirable. Unfortunately, comparative data on producer support estimates (PSE),[26] i.e., "the value of monetary transfers to agricultural production from consumers of agricultural products and from taxpayers resulting from a given set of agricultural policies in a given year," are reported beginning only in 1986. To test for the possibility that variance in agricultural support exerts an independent effect we must therefore rely on the mean level of agricultural support reported for 1990.

An economic consideration more important for policy makers may be the value of agricultural production or the chemical industry to a country's economy. One might argue that in countries where either agriculture or the chemical industry makes important contributions to GDP, or employ a significant proportion of the population, the regulation of agricultural inputs may generate greater costs. In order to capture the value of these industries to national economies, control variables reflect the average contributions to GDP of both agriculture and the chemical industry over twenty-five years.

PUBLIC OPINION   Public opinion on agrochemical regulation can cut both ways; rural interests are unlikely to support government efforts to regulate farmer behavior or increase the costs of farming. Urban dwellers, by contrast, are traditionally more likely to support government efforts to protect or improve environmental quality.

To capture the political preferences of the primary sector, we could measure the percentage of the population directly employed in agriculture or the percentage of the population living in rural areas. While sector employment offers a cleaner measure, rural population has the advantage of including many individuals who are dependent on the agricultural sector for their incomes. Rural populations also tend to hold similar political positions as those employed in agriculture, and could therefore be expected to exert political pressure in the same direction as those employed in the agricultural sector. Given that the number of people living in rural areas is larger than those directly employed in agriculture, it would also assign a greater impact to this variable, and therein a greater challenge to confirming the hypothesis. Rural population is therefore the preferred proxy for the political power of farmers.

Public opinion on environmental issues is more difficult to capture. Comparing differences in public opinion across states is always problematic, and cross-national survey data on environmental issues has a number of weaknesses. Foremost among them is that surveys conducted in the individual countries included in this study are not directly comparable, i.e., questions are not worded the same in different countries and may not actually measure preferences in a comparable way.

The most comparable data set on public preferences for environmental protection is from the World Values Surveys conducted during the early-to-mid-1990s. Researchers in this policy area often look to four survey questions about the environment for insight: respondents were asked if they agree or disagree 1) to contribute tax dollars to environmental protection, 2) to devote more income to environmental protection, 3) that government should protect environment without increases in taxes, or 4) that environmental problems are not as bad as made out to be. Arguably however, the first question is the only measure of popular opinion that is independent of previous level of government support or subjective perceptions regarding environmental quality.[27] Responses to this question alone were therefore deemed the most reliable comparative measure of public preferences for government efforts to protect the environment.

The Model

The arguments detailed above inform a model of agrochemical use that posits trends to be a product of many factors. The thesis anticipates that the institutionally induced vulnerability of politicians will affect changes in agrochemical use, controlling for changes in cropping patterns, the economic importance of agriculture and the chemical industries, the size of the rural population, and public preferences for government action to protect the environment. The vulnerability index ranges from "0" to "8" based on the vulnerability of politicians in each system as a whole, "0" being least vulnerable and "8" the most vulnerable, to quantify institutional variation. The noninstitutional variables are controlled for statistically by the inclusion of variables that measure producer subsidies, the value of the chemical industry and the primary sector to the national economy, the size of the rural population, public opinion on government responsibility to protect the environment, and changes in land area devoted to five major crops.

Methodology

The small number of countries included in the study precludes the use of individual countries as independent observations. And while cross-sectional time-series data based on annual values on each of the variables for each of the individual countries could greatly inflate the number of observations, this inflation is contraindicated by the fact that the institutional variables of theoretical interest and most control variables vary little if at all over the twenty-five-year period studied. The data on individual inputs is therefore stacked to generate four observations per country, one for each of the four pollutants, to measure changes in each of the agrochemicals used.

A stacked model offers the most analytic purchase on the question at hand because it presents an opportunity to disaggregate changes in chemical use specific to individual inputs. This is useful theoretically because policy has not targeted all agrochemicals equally; pesticides and nitrogen fertilizers pose the most dangers to the environment, phosphorus is secondary by comparison, and potash has not been identified as problematic. Given that the four measures of agrochemical pollution—pesticides, nitrogen, phosphorus, and potassium use per hectare—are simply different measures of the same dynamic, all are also subject to the same controls.

The stacked model requires that dummy variables for each of the fertilizers, nitrogen, phosphorus, and potassium, be created to test the possibility that there could be differences in their intercepts (pesticides being the base category). There is no theoretical reason to expect differences between pollutants as the data reflects percentage changes over time and not absolute values.[28] There is, however, good theoretical reason to expect that the rates of change will differ depending on the pollutant. Nitrogen fertilizers and pesticides are more serious pollutants than the other two fertilizers, and are for that reason more often the explicit targets of policies to reduce agrochemical pollution. Phosphorus has been the target of reduction measures less often, and is considered of secondary importance. Potassium is the least damaging of the group to the environment. It was therefore necessary to create interaction variables using dummies for each pollutant and the institutional index—*Index * Nitrogen, Index * Phosphorus*, and *Index * Potassium*—to test the possibility that the slopes, or rates of change, are different for each of the pollutants. An F test confirmed this expectation, and the interaction variables are therefore included in the regressions below.

DATA SOURCES FOR VARIABLES Data on changes in use for each of the agrochemicals, measured together as *Pollution Change* as described above, is from the Organization for Economic Co-operation and Development (OECD) environmental data compendiums, 1985 through 1999.[29] Data on changes in pesticide use is missing for Australia, Belgium/Luxembourg,

Canada, Iceland, and New Zealand. Thus, the maximum number of observation falls from seventy-six to seventy-one.

Nonagricultural factors are controlled for through the inclusion of six variables: *PSE* data for 1990 are also from the OECD. *WVS-Taxes* values are based on data from the World Values Survey question on willingness to devote tax dollars to environmental protection. *Rural Population* is the average proportion of the population that lived in rural areas from 1970 to 1993, based on annual World Bank data from 1970 through 1993. *Agriculture/GDP* is the contribution of agriculture to GDP, based on data from the OECD, the United Nations, and the World Bank, averaged over the same period. *Chemical Industry* is the value of the chemical industry to a country's GDP, measured as the contribution of the chemical industry to manufacturing multiplied by the contribution of manufacturing to GDP, also based on OECD, United Nations, and World Bank data. Data on both *Agriculture/GDP* and *Chemical Industry* is missing for Switzerland, therein reducing the maximum number of observations to sixty-seven.

To control for agricultural requisites, variables are also included to measure changes in land area devoted to each of the crops that may significantly impact agrochemical usage. The data for each of the variables measuring changes in land area devoted to specific crops was obtained from the United Nations' Food and Agriculture Organization (FAO).

Results

As discussed, the inclusion of variables measuring producer subsidies and popular opinion is suspect; both measurements reflect a single point in time in the mid-1990s and neither is theoretically strong. The impact of producer subsidies should be reflected in changes in crop mix, and opinion can reflect a variety of exogenous variables, including prior government actions. Nevertheless, three models are reported: one that includes a control for 1990 producer subsidies and the public's willingness to devote tax dollars to environmental protection; a second omitting the PSE variable, and finally a core model that omits both the PSE and public opinion variables.

The stacked models disaggregate the effects of the independent variable by agrochemical; the coefficient on the *Vulnerability Index* represents our estimate of the influence on the index on the use of pesticides. The coefficient on the *Vulnerability Index* must be added to the coefficient on the *Index*Nitrogen* to estimate the influence of a one-point change in the index on nitrogen use. To estimate the effects of a one-point change in the index on the use of phosphorus or potash we do the same addition: the coefficient on the *Vulnerability Index* plus the coefficient on *Index*Phosphorus* gives us our estimate of the influence of a one-point change in the index on phosphorus use; the coefficient on the *Vulnerability Index* plus the coefficient on *Index*Potash* the influence of a one-point change in the index on the use of potash.

The core model explains approximately 63 percent of the variance in pollution trends across states. The coefficients on the *Vulnerability Index* and the interaction term *Index * Nitrogen* are statistically significant

Table 3.6: Regression results—Dependent variable: rate of change in agrochemical use (1970–1995) [Coefficient (standard error) P>|t|]

	With PSE subsidy	With WVS taxes	Core model
Vulnerability index (pesticides)	.18* (.07) .013	.18* (.06) .005	.18* (.06) .005
Index/Nitrogen	.18* (.06) .006	.18* (.06) .006	.19* (.06) .005
Index/Phosphorus	−.16* (.06) .017	−.16* (.06) .016	−.15* (.06) .015
Index/Potash	−.11 (.06) .098	−.11 (.06) .095	−.11 (.06) .092
PSE	.00 (.01) .91	—	—
Public opinion	.00 (.01) .97	.00 (.01) .96	—
Rural population	.44 (1.71) .80	.43 (1.69) .80	.46 (1.63) .78
Agriculture % GDP	.08 (.05) .13	.07 (.05) .12	.07 (.04) .12
Chemical industry	.08 (.11) .48	.08 (.10) .41	.08 (.09) .34
Changes in wheat	−.02 (.04) .65	−.02 (.04) .59	−.02 (.04) .54
Changes in barley	.55* (.24) .03	.56* (.22) .02	.55* (.21) .01
Changes in potatoes	.11 (.12) .35	.12 (.10) .22	.12 (.10) .22
Changes in oilseeds	−.00 (.00) .64	−.00 (.00) .62	−.00 (.00) .60
Changes in beets	−.36 (.33) .28	−.38 (.30) .22	−.38 (.29) .20
Constant	.10 (.91) .91	.06 (.80) .94	.03 (.41) .95
N	67	67	67
R²	70	70	70
Adj. R²	62	62	63

* ≥95% confidence interval.

predictors of pesticide and nitrogen use at better than the 95-percent confidence level. The results suggest that a one-point increase in the index could account for an estimated 18-percent increase in the use of pesticides, a 37-percent increase in the use of nitrogen fertilizers (adding the coefficients on the *Vulnerability Index* and the interactive term *Index * Nitrogen:* .18 + .19 = .37), and a 3-percent increase in the use of phosphorus fertilizers over the period studied. The difference between countries located at the extreme points of the index is dramatic in both pesticide and nitrogen use. Over the twenty-five-year period studied, countries characterized by institutions that make politicians the most vulnerable to interest group demands witnessed 136 percent more pesticide use per hectare, and nearly 300 percent more nitrogen use per hectare, than countries at the other end of the institutional spectrum.

Recall that differences of this magnitude were indicated in the raw data presented above. Usage trends varied substantially across states, with countries at the low end of the index using on average only 20 percent more nitrogen in 1995 than they did in 1970, but countries at the high end of the index using on average nearly 200 percent more nitrogen in the later period, and four using approximate 400 percent more nitrogen. Differences are by contrast minimal for phosphorus, a mere 18 percent over the period, and the interactive term measuring potash sensitivity is not significant.

The relative sensitivity of these pollutants to institutionalized vulnerability is not only a reasonable expectation, but an important finding. Policies link institutions to outcomes, and policies designed to reduce the use of agrochemicals are primarily targeted at nitrogen fertilizers and pesticides. Thus, the results validate the use of interaction variables and demonstrate the usefulness of a stacked model where dependent variables differ but controls do not.

The full and partial models that include the public opinion variable are nearly identical to the core model. In no model are economic variables statistically significant predictors of agrochemical use. Of the agricultural controls, only changes in land area devoted to barley production appear to have an impact on changes in agrochemical use.

Sensitivity tests confirm that the model is robust across specifications. An increase in the index value for Finland to account for presidential effects does not alter the findings, nor does a similar increase in Italy's index value to account for its extraordinary reliance on policy making by legislative committee. The elimination of individual countries one by one does not alter the results, and expansion of the index to allow for additional index values for accountable MMD systems has no effect.

One could argue that cross-national differences in the absolute levels of agrochemical use at the beginning of the period could explain some of the variance in later trends. Some countries could arguably have a larger capacity for reduction if they were using a relatively high level of an agricultural input at the beginning of the period. By contrast, those already using relatively low levels of some input may find it more difficult to reduce their use, regardless of the fact that they would have to reduce less in absolute terms to achieve the same percentage reduction. However, a simple bivariate regression indicates that the "starting level" is not a significant indicator of later trends. Multi-variate regressions were also run with a control for the starting level of use (operationalized as the absolute level of use for each agrochemical in the beginning of the period), yet in no specification was the variable statistically significant. For those reasons it is not included here.

Discussion

The findings are clear. Cross-national differences in the reduction of agrochemical use are statistically correlated with variances in institutional design suggested by the vulnerability thesis. Moreover, the variance is substantively significant, possibly accounting for more than a 100-percent change in pesticide use and a 300-percent change in nitrogen use across the range of the index. These estimates confirm the variance found in the raw data.

Most important, the set of countries conventionally argued to be least vulnerable to interest group demands and best able to impose concentrated costs, i.e., parliamentary systems using SMD electoral systems, appear to be the least able to protect the environment in this case. This is important because this is the most significant difference between the predictions of the vulnerability thesis and those that locate interest group influence in party discipline, minority representation, or the number of veto players. All other theories suggest that if any of these causal mechanisms drove outcomes we should see the opposite effect, and the vulnerability-based model should not work. Yet international reviews of policy choice, the raw data on trends in agrochemical use, and quantitative analyses that include controls for changes in cropping patterns, economic factors, and public opinion all support the thesis.

Is it possible that the analysis presented here is wrong? Could some omitted variable be responsible for the variance? Further quantitative analysis cannot answer those questions. We must go inside these countries. The following chapters present five case studies to look for omitted variables and investigate how decisions affecting agrochemicals are made.

4

THE EUROPEAN UNION

Nowhere are the environmental impacts of agriculture as politically salient as they are in the European Union (EU). Policy makers have long recognized that the EU's Common Agricultural Policy (CAP) has had negative impacts on the environment, especially on water quality. The key issue is that EU price supports, which have been the main instrument of the CAP, generate nearly irresistible incentives for farmers to overuse chemical inputs to ensure maximum yields from scheduled crops.[1] The excessive use of agrochemicals pollutes surface water and leaches through the soil into groundwater. The resulting concerns about water quality led to multiple EU directives designed to reduce agrochemical use or ameliorate its impact, beginning with the Drinking Water Directive in 1980.

EU policies that foster or ameliorate agrochemical pollution are critical to this study because half of the democracies included in the statistical analyses in the previous chapter are members of the EU and subject to its policies. In addition, two of the countries analyzed in the following chapters were members of the EU throughout the study period, whereas two did not become members until 1995. An analysis of EU policies must therefore precede the individual country studies. This chapter provides the policy-relevant information necessary to evaluate EU-level constraints on domestic policy in subsequent chapters to ensure that cross-national differences in domestic policy choice cannot be attributed to EU-level policy. This chapter is organized into four sections. The first section describes the historical conditions that led to the CAP and the resulting policy context in which the EU and its member states combat the environmental problems associated with agricultural polices. Next we examine the policy-making processes and the EU-level environmental and agricultural policies relevant to agrochemical use in member states. The policy discussion lays the foundation necessary to evaluate the relevance of EU-level policy constraints faced by countries in the EU sphere of influence. The third section reports the results of quantitative analyses designed to assess the extent to which policies may have affected member state actions and therein cross-national variance in the trends of agrochemical use. The chapter concludes with a discussion of policy variance among EU member states and the possible effect of EU policies on the specific determinants of agrochemical use identified in the previous chapter.

Agriculture and the Environment in the European Union

The greatest influence on agricultural decisions in the member states of the EU, including the use of agrochemicals, is arguably the CAP, which has long been criticized for its economic inefficiencies and environmental impacts. The price support system created financial incentives for all member states to increase production regardless of the consequences.[2] Substantial food surpluses generated high costs to store the fabled "wine lakes" and "butter mountains" that could not be sold even with expensive export subsidies, and forced the regular destruction of good fruits and vegetables. As the value of land jumped, large numbers of farmers sold their property, and Europe's cherished family farms were increasingly consolidated into large commercial enterprises. To add insult to injury, target prices higher than the world market forced EU citizens to pay more for their food than they would have paid otherwise, and the high levels of agrochemical use continue to threaten drinking water quality. To put the policy responses to these problems in context we must consider the historical and political factors that ushered in and maintained a policy that was so tremendously costly.

The Common Market and the Common Agricultural Policy

Much of the European countryside was destroyed during World War II, and consequently European agricultural production was severely

depressed and large numbers of Europeans were underfed and malnour-
ished. Farmers left their land for the cities in hope of finding work, adding
to the already overwhelming social burden faced by city governments in
the postwar environment. In response, all European governments created
incentives to entice farmers to stay on their land and produce food in
quantities sufficient to feed the population at reasonable prices.

Against this backdrop, leaders in Belgium, France, Germany,
Luxembourg, Italy, and the Netherlands entered into discussions to create
a common market that they hoped would bind the countries together so
tightly it would discourage future wars. While initial discussions focused on
the creation of a common market in manufactured goods, it soon became
clear that eliminating tariffs on manufactured goods would have generated
disproportional benefits for Germany, because its economy was the most
heavily dependent on manufacturing. A common market in agricultural
products was needed to provide commensurate benefits for France, which
relied heavily on the agricultural sector for its contribution to employment
and the economy.[3] This made prior commitment to a common agricultural
policy integral to France's agreement to the 1957 Treaty of Rome, which
created the European Economic Community (EEC), what later became
the EU.

Given the agricultural situation across Europe in the 1950s, the goals
of the proposed policy were simple and noncontroversial. Article 39
of the Treaty of Rome stipulated that the future CAP should be designed
to increase agricultural productivity, ensure a fair standard of living for
farmers, stabilize markets, and provide a dependable supply of food
for the domestic market at reasonable prices. In 1962, after more than
four years of intense negotiations, the EEC's Council of Agricultural
Ministers, the legislative body with decision-making authority over
agricultural matters, agreed to a package of policy instruments designed
to achieve these goals. The EEC adopted target, threshold, and intervention prices; export subsides; a common external tariff; and variable
import levies. Agricultural prices and levies were to be set annually by the
Council. Import levies would vary to bring the cost of imports to the
threshold price, and the tariffs were expected to pay for the cost of
export subsidies. Intervention prices—the rates at which the European
Commission, the executive arm of the EEC, would buy food to take it

off the market—set the floor of the domestic market and were designed to provide the guaranteed prices necessary to generate investment, secure farm loans, and provide farmers with a decent standard of living. Export subsidies, officially called "refunds," reimbursed farmers for the difference between the lower world market price and the EU price for a commodity.

At the same time that policy makers were enacting policies to increase agricultural production, the agricultural sector was undergoing a dramatic transformation that negated the need for these policies. The mechanization of agricultural production and the advent of chemical pesticides developed during the war allowed farmers to apply inputs by machine. The economies of scale necessary to rationalize investment in large machinery generated incentives for farmers to shift from mixed farming (planting multiple crops and raising livestock) to mono-cropping (farming a single crop over a large area). This structural change increased the use of synthetic fertilizers and pesticides exponentially and allowed farmers to grow more food on less land and at a lower cost.

International negotiations over the creation of the common market in agricultural products that insulated European farmers from overseas competition also affected the use of agrochemicals. In anticipation of common external tariffs on commodities, negotiations during the Kennedy Round of General Agreement on Tariffs and Trade (GATT) allowed animal feed to be imported from the United States with zero or minimal tariff.[4] The availability of low-cost animal feed helped concentrate European livestock production near the ports, depriving inland areas of manure and thereby increasing the need for chemical fertilizers.[5]

The economic incentives of the CAP, the GATT agreement on animal feed, and sector modernization combined to create sometimes severe agricultural pollution, especially from synthetic nitrogen fertilizers and excess nitrogen from animal manure. By the 1990s regional water quality in most member states exceeded the EU and World Health Organization (WHO) maximum standard for nitrates. The best data suggest that at this time 22 percent of European groundwater had concentrations above the maximum level of 50 mg/l (milligrams per liter), and 87 percent exceeded the EU- and WHO-recommended level of 25 mg/l.[6]

Policies Affecting Agrochemical Use

Unlike policy making in domestic arenas, EU policies are made by decision makers whose competencies are limited to a specific policy sector. Policy proposals originate in sector-specific Directorates General (DGs) of the European Commission, which resemble functional executive ministries in parliamentary democracies. Policy proposals are then sent to the relevant sector-specific Council of Ministers, which is made up of the relevant ministers from member states, and a sector-specific committee of the European Parliament (EP), the only popularly elected EU body. The Council of Ministers has long been considered the most important legislative body of the EU, but the EP has gained power over time. Notably, however, the EP's power has developed unevenly, with substantially more power in some policy sectors than others. This is relevant here because the EP power in agricultural policy is quite low, whereas its power in environmental policy is quite high.

Environmental Policies

The EU policies adopted to address agrochemical pollution of water supplies include the Drinking Water Directive of 1980 and the Nitrate Directive of 1991. These directives represent the most significant EU efforts designed to affect fertilizer and pesticide use or to ameliorate their effects. The initiation of these and other environmental directives is the purview of the Directorate General on Environment (formerly known as DG XI), the department within the European Commission with the responsibility to initiate environmental policy. Environmental policies proposed by the Commission's Environment DG are debated and largely decided by member state representatives in the Council of Environmental Ministers and the EP environment committee. Therefore, like other EU policies, both of the EU directives reviewed here were made in relative isolation from other interests, even those of agriculture. This point is important because many argue that the segregation of policy making allowed environmental interests to enact extremely stringent water quality limits that were later viewed as inappropriate and unachievable.

THE DRINKING WATER DIRECTIVE (80/778) The earliest directive to address agrochemical pollution is the 1980 Drinking Water Directive (80/778), which dictates a maximum level for nitrates of 50 mg/l, and a "guide level" (the level member states should seek) of 25 mg/l. The Directive also dictates a maximum value of .1 g/l (micrograms per liter) for each pesticide in drinking water, and a "cocktail" maximum of .5 g/l for all pesticides combined.[7] When the Directive was enacted, these levels were surrogates for a zero, as equipment did not yet exist to detect such minute levels of contamination.

Several aspects of this Directive affect the policy responses of member states. First, the maximum levels chosen for pesticides were not a product of scientific consensus or even of scientific advice. It was not the case that every pesticide found in drinking water in excess of .1 g/l was known to be dangerous to humans. Indeed, we may ingest many more times this amount of some pesticides through residues found on food. Nor is it possible that all substances are equally toxic, and therefore equally dangerous at the .1 g/l level.

Second, the .1- g/l and .5- g/l levels for pesticides are almost irrelevant in the face of agrochemical development over the past twenty years. In the 1970s pesticides were applied in kilograms per hectare, and the maximum levels dictated in the Drinking Water Directive were a response to that situation. By the time the Directive went into effect new products were applied in grams per hectare. As a result, one could argue that even if the levels were not arbitrary in the first place, they became inappropriate and potentially dangerous once in place.

Third, the Directive targets water suppliers rather than the users or manufacturers of fertilizers and pesticides. As a result, the Directive has imposed the burden of ameliorating agrochemical pollution on water suppliers and their consumers, rather than on those who create the pollution. Water companies in some parts of England and Germany, for example, pay farmers not to use certain pesticides at all, or not to use pesticides in sensitive areas.[8] Some large water suppliers install very costly granular activated carbon filters (GAC) instead, which cannot remove nitrate but can remove some, (not all), pesticides. Some companies stop using water too contaminated with pesticides, cap the old wells and drill new; some simply mix contaminated water with cleaner water before delivering it to the public.

Whatever the method, however, water suppliers and consumers ultimately pay to decontaminate drinking water or locate uncontaminated supplies.

Each of these factors contributed to implementation problems. The most important is arguably the fact that the Directive lacks credibility with those affected. Farmers, pesticide manufacturers, extension service advisors, policy makers, as well as scientists all recognize that pesticides are not equally dangerous and should not be regulated as if they were. Carney (1991) suggests that the credibility issue underpins member state reluctance to enact the legislation necessary to make the Directive effective. He finds that the states that do enact legislation often exempt certain substances from measurement, assign certain substances guide levels rather than maximums, or set less stringent maximum levels for specific pollutants. And while member states are required to report when pollutants exceed maximum allowable levels, many states apparently report only those violations related to known health concerns.[9]

Additional reporting problems arise from the fact that member states use a wide variety of techniques to measure water quality. The Environment Directorate cannot mitigate these implementation problems because it lacks the funds and institutional infrastructure to monitor compliance. As a result, self-reporting by member states has been inadequate to gauge compliance and determine changes in water contamination.

THE NITRATE DIRECTIVE (91/676) The 1991 Nitrate Directive, the second environmental directive to address agricultural pollution, has proven even more difficult to implement and has been the most expensive environmental directive for member states. As the name implies, the Directive targets nitrogen pollution alone, reaffirming the maximum level of 50 mg/l of nitrates in surface and groundwater set by the Drinking Water Directive. The key additional requirement is that member states must identify areas, called "nitrate vulnerable zones," where water supplies are at risk of exceeding the limit, and institute "action plans" to address the pollution.

The Directive was not achievable during the study period. No member state had fully complied with all programs, and all EU assessments of the Directive suggest that compliance may be impossible. Reporting requirements also proved expensive for the member states. At least one member state was brought before the European Court of Justice for failing to implement the directive.

Agricultural Policies

The Agriculture Directorate enacted two directives that had the potential to affect agrochemical use in member states: the 1991 Plant Protection Directive and the 1992 Agri-Environmental Measures. Unlike directives originating in the Environment Directorate, both measures had the potential (if not the intent) to address the sources of agrochemical pollution. Like environmental policies, however, agricultural policies are made in relative isolation from nonagricultural interests. Agricultural policy originates in the Commission's Directorate General on Agriculture, (formerly known as DG-VI), and is then debated and often decided by the Council of Agriculture Ministers. In contrast to its growing power in other areas, including environmental policy, the EP's power over agriculture was limited during the study period to giving its formal written position, called its "Opinion." The EP may exert some power if it chooses to withhold its Opinion, but once it is delivered neither the Council nor the Commission is required to act on it.

THE EU PLANT PROTECTION DIRECTIVE (91/414) The Agriculture Directorate's Plant Protection Directive (PPD) was motivated by the desire to harmonize registration processes across member states so chemical companies need only prepare one data package for all of Europe. It is difficult to measure the impact of the "Plant Protection Products" regulation, given the slow speed at which it has been implemented. In 1991, the stated goal of the Directive was to review ninety of the over nine hundred active ingredients on the market each year for ten years. However, none of the active agreements were listed on Annex I, the accepted list of active ingredients reviewed and available for use in the member states, by the end of the study period.

AGRI-ENVIRONMENTAL MEASURES (2078/92) The final policy potentially relevant to agrochemical use in member states came with the 1992 MacSharry reforms of the CAP. As indicated above, the CAP has been almost immune to reform. These reforms were possible only in the face of a pending budgetary crisis and substantial trade pressures to liberalize the sector during the Uruguay Round.[10] The reforms reduced price supports, created direct compensatory payments, mandated set-asides, and introduced the "agri-environmental" measures (2078/92). The agri-environmental measures have the potential to reduce agrochemical pollution via a host of subsidies for more environmentally benign agricultural production. The measures provide funds which member states may choose to use for programs that encourage farmers to reduce agrochemical use and agriculture's environmental impact. Importantly, however, agri-environmental monies may also provide funds to maintain hedgerows, rebuild stone walls, or refurbish culturally valuable structures. The choice belongs to the member state. Table 4.1 demonstrates the different patterns of uptake and design of these programs have resulted in radical differences between states.

Importantly, there are also qualitative differences between state programs that cannot be seen in the data. For example, Finland requires that farmers meet very strict requirements to receive payments under 2078. This fact

Table 4.1. Agri-environmental program (2078/92) participation distribution (%)

	Farmers involved	Land in programs	Utilizing organic	Environmental improvement	Low intensity subsidies	Environmental management	Farmer training
Austria	67	72	17	59	21	3	0
Belgium	1	1	20	58	5	14	3
Denmark	7	3	24	46	16	14	0
Finland	59	77	5	42	42	7	5
France	16	19	3	15	79	3	1
Germany	46	37	1	56	21	21	1
Iceland							
Ireland	17	18	2	49	21	24	4
Italy	4	6	23	43	22	10	2
Luxembourg	32	76	1	39	56	3	0
Netherlands	2	2	2	32	0	0	66
Sweden	56	45	15	6	71	1	7
U.K.	4	8	2	53	30	14	0

Source: EU Commission (1997).

is significant given that 80 percent of its farmers are covered under these schemes. By contrast, countries like France appear to use 2078 funds to support existing activities, like maintenance of low input systems. The data also obscures the fact that some premiums can be increased by the member states to further stimulate change, and some programs require that member states provide up to 50 percent of the funding for program measures. Opportunities for member state enhancement may advantage richer states over poorer states, and may therefore explain a portion of the differential rates of uptake.

Given the variance in program design and funding, the environmental impacts of the programs vary across states. However, most observers argue that the monitoring and enforcement of 2078 programs is generally inadequate, the environmental impact is often either insignificant or not different from good agricultural practice, the administrative burden on member states is very high, and, as a result, agri-environmental measures are ultimately insignificant with respect to pollution control.[11] This is not unexpected given that only 3 percent of the CAP budget is allocated for all agri-environmental schemes, and these small subsidies compete with the same incentives that intensified agrochemical use in the first place. One has to wonder what net effect they could conceivably have on agrochemical pollution.

Most important to the subsequent case studies, while none of the agri-environmental measures require member states to impose costs on farmers or agrochemical manufacturers, they did provide member states with EU funds to pay farmers not to pollute, should they choose to do so.

Differences Between Member and Nonmember States

The potential significance of EU agricultural and environmental policies suggests that we should control for the possibility that EU membership may affect cross-national differences in agrochemical use. To test that proposition, we can conduct the same quantitative analysis as in the previous chapter with a control for EU membership to measure its independent effect on trends. As in the previous chapter, regression results are reported for all three models: one with controls for cross-national differences in agricultural subsidies and public preferences for government effort to protect the environment, a second without the control for subsidies—a control that may hide the influence the Common Agricultural Policy, and a third "core" model without controls for environmental preferences or subsidy levels.

Comparing the results of the regressions in Table 4.2 with their counterparts reported in Table 3.3, we find only trivial differences in the size of coefficients of theoretical interest or their statistical significance. The significant difference in agrochemical use among advanced democracies

Table 4.2. Regression results—Dependent variable: rate of change in agrochemical use (1970–1995) [Coefficient (standard error) P>|t|]

	With PSE subsidy	With WVS taxes	Core model
Vulnerability index (pesticides)	.19* (.07) .012	.18* (.06) .005	.18* (.06) .005
Index / Nitrogen	.19* (.06) .006	.19* (.06) .005	.19* (.06) .005
Index / Phosphorus	–.15* (.06) .021	–.15* (.06) .020	–.15* (.06) .018
Index / Potash	–.10 (.06) .115	–.10 (.06) .110	–.10 (.06) .107
Producer subsidies (PSE)	.00 (.01) .89	—	—
Public opinion (taxes)	.00 (.01) .99	.00 (.01) .99	—
EU membership	.14 (.25) .57	.13 (.23) .57	.13 (.23) .57
Rural population	.47 (1.73) .79	.46 (1.70) .79	.46 (1.63) .78
Agriculture % GDP	.07 (.05) .16	.07 (.04) .13	.07 (.05) .12
Chemical industry	.05 (.11) .67	.04 (.11) .68	.05 (.10) .66
Changes in wheat	-.02 (.04) .60	-.02 (.03) .60	–.02 (.04) .58
Changes in barley	.56* (.24) .02	.54* (.22) .02	.55* (.21) .01
Changes in potatoes	.11 (.12) .38	.10 (.11) .37	.10 (.10) .35
Changes in oilseeds	–.00 (.00) .52	–.00 (.00) .52	–.00 (.00) .50
Changes in beets	–.37 (.33) .27	–.35 (.31) .26	–.35 (.30) .24
Constant	–.01 (.94) .99	.05 (.81) .95	.05 (.41) .91
N	67	67	67
R²	70	70	70
Adj. R²	62	62	63

* ≥ 95 percent confidence interval.

is not due to EU membership. As in the model without a control for EU membership, a one-unit increase in the Index value generates an approximately 18 percent increase in pesticide use and a 37 percent increase in nitrogen use over the twenty-five-year period. The original findings are robust. Domestic institutions remain the variable that best explains differences in agrochemical use across states.

Conclusion

EU policies are widely viewed as having a significant impact on the environmental problems associated with agriculture. Yet the policy review above and the quantitative analysis that followed found no effect on the primary environmental problem associated with agriculture—agrochemical use that leads to water pollution. While surprising, the finding is easily explained: All of the policies identified by international agencies as the critical determinants of agrochemical use (i.e., taxes, farmer education, machine certification, and chemical regulation) lie outside EU control. As important as it is, the Common Agricultural Policy is "common" only in its economic instruments, i.e., price supports, export subsides, etc. Farmer education, farm equipment regulations, state-supported extension services, and the design of agri-environmental programs differ substantially across states.

However, cross-national differences visible in the raw data on agrochemical trends are consistent with cross-national variation in the uptake by individual member states of EU agri-environmental measures and the faithful implementation of EU environmental directives generally.[12] Scholars who study environmental performance generally argue that member states fall into one of three groups: those that are considered "environmental leaders" because they prefer stronger environmental policies, those that are generally neutral, and those considered "environmental laggards," i.e., they fight strengthening environmental policies in general. Of the member states included in this study, Austria, Denmark, Germany, Finland, the Netherlands, and Sweden constitute the first group; Belgium, France, Italy, and Luxembourg the second; Ireland and the United Kingdom the third.[13] Environmental leaders generally implement EU directives quickly and faithfully; laggards often fail to implement EU policy. This is certainly born out in this case: those member states that are least compliant have experienced increases in agricultural pollution; those that are most compliant have achieved significant reductions.

This suggests two things. First, it suggests that ultimate differences in agrochemical use may reflect the legal nature of EU directives. Directives are distinct from regulations because they bind member states to goals and objectives without dictating the means to accomplishing those ends. Consequently, each government must choose how to structure programs funded by the EU, in this case how to regulate agricultural activities not governed by the CAP, and how to protect the environment from agricultural pollution more generally.

Second, the consistencies also suggest that domestic institutions explain member state behavior domestically and at the EU level. These categorizations of member states as environmental leaders and laggards are also consistent with the vulnerability thesis. All those included in the first group use proportional representation (PR) electoral systems, and all but one use pure PR; only Germany uses a mixed-member system. Those in the second group include one that uses majority rule (France) and another that used open list PR (Italy), and two countries that use PR (Belgium and Luxembourg). Included in the group of laggards is one country that uses SMD (United Kingdom) and one that uses a highly accountable MMD (Ireland).

As indicated in the previous chapter, the proof is in the policy. The link between differences in outcomes and formal political institutions is in specific policy choices. To explore those differences, the following chapters present four in-depth cases studies that link policy choice to outcomes. Given common environmental goals and the common agricultural policy constraints emanating from the CAP, it is interesting to survey the differences in domestic policy in two member states and two nonmember states. Two questions direct our focus: First, do policies enacted impose concentrated costs on powerful interest groups? And second, is it reasonable to conclude that the imposition of costs can be credited with differences in observed trends in agrochemical use?

5

THE UNITED KINGDOM: MINORITY INFLUENCE AND MAJORITY RULE

Models that link minority influence to political institutions that fragment political power suggest that interest groups should be the least powerful where single-member district (SMD) elections are combined with parliamentary government and a unitary organization of the state. The vulnerability thesis predicts the opposite; it anticipates that policy makers in these systems will be the most vulnerable to the demands of small groups. The United Kingdom was selected for the first case study because the British political system is defined by this particular institutional constellation and is therefore a critical case.

SMD elections empower three significant parties in Britain: the Conservatives, the Labour Party, and the Liberal Democrats. While the Liberal Democrats often win more than 20 percent of the vote, the winner-take-all electoral system allows them to claim less than 10 percent of the seats on average. Plurality rules tend to award one of the two larger parties with more seats than their proportion of the vote, normally allowing one party to govern alone with a majority of parliamentary seats, even though no party has won a majority of the vote since World War II.[1] The electoral system's tendency to "manufacture majorities" from a mere plurality of votes is especially important in Britain, a parliamentary regime with a unitary state structure, because all political power in Britain resides in the national parliament. This allows the majority party in parliament to select the executive and govern without the need to compromise with other parties, an independently elected executive, or lower levels of government. Given that policy originates in the executive in parliamentary systems, and most policy is easily passed by a party vote in the legislature, policy-making power is more concentrated in this system than in any other type of democracy.

Conventional theories predict that this concentration of political power in a single party at the national level will insulate British policy makers from the demands of small groups. If true, the British government should be able to impose concentrated costs on powerful minorities when necessary to achieve its chosen policy goals. If the British government cannot achieve its goals, however, and if the reason for its failure can be traced to the inability to impose concentrated costs, the vulnerability of highly identifiable British governments and the highly accountable politicians on which they rest may be to blame.

This case study, like those that follow, is organized into three parts. The first section explores the linkages between institutional structure and policy choice in the United Kingdom. We begin with a brief description of the agricultural situation in the U.K. before and during the study period and then examine the major policies directed at agrochemical use, focusing particular attention on the role of EU directives in British policy initiatives. The second section moves from the halls of parliament to farmers' fields to identify all nongovernmental determinants of agrochemical use to investigate the possibility that unforeseen factors may be influencing outcomes. The final section concludes with a discussion of the U.K. in comparative perspective and alternative explanations for British governments' behavior.

Agriculture and the Environment in Britain

The 1947 Agricultural Act marked the beginning of guaranteed prices and modern agriculture in Britain. War-time food shortages drove government efforts to increase agricultural production to ensure self-sufficiency in food production and low prices. To that end, the British government created the Agricultural Development and Advisory Service (ADAS) to conduct research on improving yields and to advise British farmers on how to intensify production through the use of chemicals and new technology. Technological modernization during the 1950s and 1960s accelerated those efforts and facilitated rapid increases in agrochemical use because new machinery generated incentives for specialization that made the use of chemicals more efficient. Chemical inputs became an important factor of production almost overnight, a rare and welcome control for a sector normally vulnerable to the vagaries of both pests and climate. With the U.K. accession to the European Community (EC) in 1973, the high target prices of the Common Agricultural Policy (CAP) provided strong economic incentives to maximize yields. These three forces combined to generate dramatic changes in the farming structure that encouraged specialization and intense agrochemical use.

By the time Rachel Carson's book *Silent Spring* ignited alarm over the environmental impact of pesticides, the die had already been cast. Reductions in agrochemical use went against the advice of the agricultural extension service, the incentives of the CAP, and the efficient use of agricultural land in a time of rapid technological and chemical development. Moreover, no incentives to reduce agrochemical use were forthcoming from the British government. Despite the fact that the size of the farming population shrank and food shortages gave way to food surpluses, policies designed to increase production were maintained as if nothing had changed.

Interest Groups and Policy Choice

Policies that affect agrochemical use have long been made by a closed community consisting of the Ministry of Agriculture, Fisheries and Food (MAFF), the National Farmers Union (NFU), and the agrochemical industry. The NFU is by far the most significant nongovernmental actor in policy choice. In the words of a leading scholar on British politics, "The National Farmers Union is a classic example of an insider interest group; it enjoys such a close relationship with the Ministry of Agriculture that most agricultural policy in Britain is made jointly by the ministry and the farmers' union leaders."[2] The NFU is powerful because it gained a near monopoly on farmers' representation even before the war. Many farmers viewed membership as compulsory because the NFU lobbied on behalf of farmers and provided valuable fringe benefits with membership, including insurance and legal services.[3] Its membership rolls and its ability to speak for all farmers earned it the ear of the agricultural ministry and thus the government.

Policies Affecting the Use of Agrochemicals

When environmental concerns threatened the policy dominance of MAFF and the NFU in the mid-1980s, the NFU worked to protect the role of MAFF in all environmental policies affecting agriculture. The NFU successfully coopted the environment as a political issue and promoted itself and MAFF as advocates of environmental goods in agriculture.[4] Winter argues that their primary goal was to establish farmers' property rights to the countryside at the outset, and thus the need for compensatory payments when the environmentally damaging activities of conventional agriculture were forgone (1996:227). This principle was established with the creation of the "Environmentally Sensitive Areas" (ESA) scheme introduced in 1987. The MAFF program defined ESAs as those where "traditional agriculture" must be employed for conservation purposes and farmers must be compensated for environmentally responsible agriculture. The voluntary scheme compensated farmers if they agreed to preserve historic landscape features or restrict their use of agrochemicals.[5] This single voluntary program was the one and only domestically initiated program designed to reduce agrochemical use during the entire twenty-five-year study period.

EUROPEAN UNION DIRECTIVES The bulk of British efforts toward environmentally sustainable agriculture were in response to directives taken by the European Community (EC) and what later became the European Union (EU). As a member of the EU Britain was a signatory to the 1980 Drinking Water Directive (DWD) and the 1991 Nitrate Directive reviewed in the previous chapter.

The Drinking Water Directive (80/778) The EC directive on drinking water quality was first proposed in 1975. In an effort to determine the current and anticipated levels of nitrates in the U.K., the British government undertook a study of surface and groundwater quality at that time.[6] That study found that some British water supplies were already contaminated well in excess of the proposed 50 mg/l limit, and the study's authors predicted additional water supplies would exceed the maximum level over the following two decades as nitrogen already in the soil leached into aquifers. The figures used to generate these estimates were conservative. Although the British government was aware of the dramatic increase in fertilizer use at the time of the study (400 percent from 1950 to 1970), the model that predicted future levels assumed that use would remain stagnant at the 1970 level. Nevertheless, the U.K. agreed to the DWD in 1980, and therein its implementation by 1985.

Given poor British water quality relative to the new EC standards, one might expect the British government to enact policies to reduce agrochemical use at the source. Yet it did not. Rather than require farmers to use fewer inputs or use them more judiciously, the government focused on compliance by the end user, transferring the costs of meeting EC standards to water suppliers and consumers. The justification was economic; the government argued that remedial measures used by the Regional Water Authorities were a more cost-effective way to treat drinking water. When well water did not meet DWD requirements, water suppliers were expected to blend it with less-contaminated water, drill deeper bore holes, store the contaminated water in reservoirs to allow microbiological de-nitrification, or simply stop using the contaminated well. If all else failed, suppliers were expected to provide consumers tanker or bottled water.[7]

The only piece of legislation enacted to implement the DWD, the Code of Good Agricultural Practice, came in 1985, the final date by which the British government agreed to implement the DWD. While ostensibly an instrument of pollution control, it was designed by the Ministry of Agriculture, not the Environment Agency. Importantly, the code did not impose constraints on farmers' behavior, but instead merely formalized standard practices. Consequently, some argue that the most important function of the code was its ability to protect farmers from legal prosecution under the 1974 Control of Pollution Act if they could show that they observed the code.[8]

Despite European legislation directing the British government to effect change, legislation to which the government was itself a party, the government did not impose restrictions on agrochemical use. Instead, MAFF launched a second voluntary program, the Nitrate Sensitive Areas Scheme, which offered farmers in "Nitrate Sensitive Areas" (NSAs) the opportunity to enter voluntary agreements to restrict nitrogen use in exchange for compensatory payments. The program began in 1990 with the creation of ten NSAs, and was expanded to thirty-two areas across the U.K. in 1994. Farmers located within the designated areas who wanted to participate agreed to employ certain farming methods or to take arable land out of production to reduce nitrate leaching in exchange for government payments. The generosity of compensatory payments was evidenced by the fact that despite the voluntary nature of the program, 87 percent of the land within the NSAs was entered into the scheme.[9] Several methods employed in the scheme were quite effective in reducing nitrate leaching; the cover crop scheme, for example, was accredited with reducing nitrate loss by 50 percent.

The Nitrate Directive (91/676) The next phase of government activity was in response to the development of an EC directive on nitrates. In early 1989, a draft of what would become the EU Nitrate Directive was issued. It proposed that nitrogen use be severely restricted in all areas where waters might be polluted by nitrogen fertilizers above the maximum acceptable level.[10] The directive called for the identification of "Nitrate Vulnerable Zones" (NVZs), and "action plans" to reduce nitrate leaching from agriculture in those zones.

Nothing is as illustrative of the U.K.'s reluctance to impose costs on farmers as the development of NVZs. In a complicated and drawn-out process, unlike any in other member states, the designation of NVZs in the U.K. limited the land included by every means possible. As a result of its attempt to minimize the number of zones, the European Commission brought the U.K. before the European Court of Justice in February 1999 to defend its determination of NVZs. The Commission argued that the British government failed to implement the Directive properly, and, in July 2000, the court found in favor of the Commission.

The problem started with the first step in the designation process. As a response to MAFF pressure to minimize the number of NVZs, the government began the designation process by limiting eligibility to aquifers that were the source of existing public water supplies.[11] This initial decision was problematic because the directive was not limited to public water supplies, nor was it limited to aquifers that were the source of water supplies at the time.

The second step was to determine the location of NVZs within this limited area. To that end, the government began collecting historical water quality information and checking suspect bore holes for contamination. Using this data, existing nitrate levels were determined and trends were predicted. If nitrate levels were above the 50-mg/l level, or if the 50-mg/l level would be reached by 2010 based on trends revealed by the data, the area was a candidate NVZ. The data collection and mathematical modeling process took approximately five years to complete.

Once maps of groundwater contamination by nitrates were made, areas that were 30 percent or more urban were excluded from designation. The government argued that farmers' use of nitrogen should not be curtailed in these areas because urban populations may have contributed to the nitrate contamination through leaking sewers. The argument was extended to any area where nitrate could come from some other source, e.g., deicing on airport runways, allowing agricultural acreage to be excluded if it was not the sole source of nitrogen for the water supply.

In the last step of the process these preliminary maps of vulnerable zones were overlaid on maps outlining the borders of actual farms to iden-tify the ownership of individual farms to be included in each NVZ. The Environment Agency then consulted with the identified farmers to explain its methodology. If a farmer believed the designation to be in error, he or she had the right to request a written response addressing the concern. In some instances the Environment Agency visited the farm as well. If the farmer and the agency ultimately disagreed, the farmer had the right to appeal to a panel within MAFF. The entire process took an average of three to four years. In 1995, the panel found that the Environment Agency had not calculated pollution trends correctly. Per the panel's direction, the Agency had to recalculate trends using a different statistical method and then redesignate the NVZs accordingly.

When the zones were redesignated, the government's "Action Plan" for the newly determined zones was finally instituted in December of 1998. It requires that farmers do not apply *manufactured* nitrogen fertilizer:

- to flooded, waterlogged, frozen "hard," or snow covered land
- between September 15 and February 1 for grass, and between September 1 and February 1 for fields not in grass *unless there is a specific crop requirement during that time* (emphasis added).
- to steeply sloping fields (no angle given)

- in excess of crop requirements
- in such a way as they are likely to enter directly into surface waters

Arguably, nearly a decade of intense government effort resulted in regulations that do not go beyond simple common sense, and do not differ substantively from the 1985 Code of Good Agricultural Practice adopted before the process began.

Pesticide Regulation and the Plant Protection Products Directive (91/414) The only domestic legislation to regulate pesticides is the 1986 Control of Pesticides Regulations. Prior to that time two voluntary schemes were the sole components of the domestic approval system. The 1957 Pesticides Safety Precautions Scheme (PSPS), governed by the Advisory Committee on Pesticides (APC), evaluated products in terms of human (operator) safety. The 1960 Agricultural Chemical Approval Scheme (ACAS) run by MAFF evaluated the efficacy of new products, i.e., whether they produced the results stated on the label. Environmental impact was not a consideration of either scheme.[12]

When the EC adopted the Plant Protection Products Directive in 1991, the British government chose to discontinue the nascent domestic process for new products.[13] Given that no active substances were listed in Annex I by the end of the study period, there were no environmental restrictions on the use of pesticides during this time.

CAP Reform and Agri-environmental Measures (2078/92) As indicated in the previous chapter, the agri-environmental measures made funds available to member states to facilitate a reduction in agrochemical use. By the end of 1995, only 4 percent of British farmers participated in the agri-environmental programs and, of those, 97 percent were in "Environmental Management," "Environmental Improvement," or "Low Intensity Subsidies."[14] In laymen terms, these schemes are largely directed at aesthetic or what is more commonly referred to as "land-scape issues"—i.e., the preservation or re-creation of hedgerows and the maintenance or refurbishing of outdated (and nonfunctional) barns. The only program that had a potential to impact the use of agrochemicals was the Organic Aid scheme, but only 2 percent of the 4 percent of farmers participating in agri-environmental program took part in the organic scheme, far too few to have a measurable effect. Moreover, none of the EU agri-environmental measures used in Britain reduced agrochemical usage on conventional farms,[15] and there was no participation in EU's agri-environmental programs devoted to farmer education during the study period.

British Policy Choice in Theoretical Context

As indicated in chapter three, all empirical measures related to the use of agrochemicals in the U.K. are consistent with a vulnerability-based model of interest group influence. In terms of raw usage levels, per hectare nitrogen use has shown a near steady rise since 1970, more than doubling by 1995. Of the fourteen other European countries studied, this increase is larger than all other states except Ireland and Italy.

The inability to reduce agrochemical pollution is not surprising given the policy environment. This case study confirms that British policy instruments have imposed no restrictions on farmers or chemical distributors. While agricultural policies are designed through close cooperation between government and vested agricultural interests in most countries, only the U.K. relies entirely on voluntary compliance to meet environmental goals.[16] Moreover, the policy history described above reveals that most of the voluntary schemes that do exist were driven by the need to comply with EU directives. Finally, all voluntary programs pay farmers not to pollute, in conflict with the U.K.'s own "Polluter Pays Principle."[17]

The Determinants of Agrochemical Use

Given the dearth of government policies in this area, it is important to look for other factors that may influence a farmer's use of pesticides or fertilizer. To that end, interviews were conducted with representatives of the NFU, the British Agrochemical Association, the National Center on Ecotoxicology, the Royal Society for the Protection of Birds, representatives of the Linking Environment and Farming program (LEAF), and British farmers across the country. Interviewees consistently identified the same three primary determinants of British farmers' usage of agrochemicals: the prices of crops as dictated by the CAP, supermarket and miller protocols, and, most important, the advice of "crop-walkers."

The role played by the CAP in agrochemical use was discussed in the previous chapter, therefore I will not repeat that discussion here. Suffice it to say that the CAP affects crop prices for all member states, and the statistical analyses reported in the previous chapter clearly show that subsidy levels and EU membership do not explain cross-national trends in agrochemical use. The heavy reliance on crop-walkers and the influence of supermarket protocols are, however, unique to Britain and, as such, demand our attention.

Crop-Walkers

The single most important domestic determinant of agrochemical use in the U.K. is the face-to-face advice individual farmers receive from their crop-walkers. Prior to and during the study period, the vast majority of farmers relied exclusively on crop-walkers, who personally walk farmers' fields and advise them on their crops' needs for chemical inputs. Crop-walkers generally have long and close relationships with the farmers they service, and farmers rely on their crop-walkers to protect their crops from pests and maximize yields. Crop-walkers may work for the government advisory service (ADAS) or for a chemical distributor, or for self-employed contractors, referred to as "independents." Importantly, however, all three groups are trained, at least in part, by the agrochemical industry. Advisors generally receive 80–110 hours of industry training per year. The nature of the training differs by company, but approximately 70 percent has a product focus, and 30 percent is on farm management.[18]

Those farmers that use independents pay a fee for their service and then purchase the recommended chemicals from large suppliers at a lower cost. Only farmers of the largest farms, perhaps 30 percent of the total, utilized independents. With the 1986 Agriculture Act, ADAS crop-walkers also began to charge a fee for advice. As ADAS had been designed to provide advice on how to increase production, the government argued that there was no reason to continue its funding in an era of surpluses.[19] The impact of the change was quite small, however, as the majority of British farmers never relied on ADAS for agrochemical advice. According to a longtime British farmer, farmers believe that if the ADAS advisors were good at their jobs they would work for a distributor because the pay is better; if they were very good they would become Independents, whose income reflects ability and reputation.[20] Thus, the vast majority of British farmers, approximately 60 to 70 percent, have traditionally relied on chemical distributors for agrochemical advice.[21] The advice of chemical distributors has always been, and continues to be, free of charge—as long as farmers purchase their products from that distributor.

The use of chemical distributors rather than independent advisors is one of the most important differences between the farmers of small and large farms in the U.K. Obviously, distributors are in the business of selling chemicals, and their success is based on their ability to recommend chemicals that maximize yields and minimize risk. Farmers do not expect chemical distributors to advise them on how to protect the environment. In fact, according to a former distributor employee, financial incentives are such that one can expect that distributors provide little or no information on alternatives to chemicals, just alternative chemicals.[22] It is also reasonable to expect that if there are overstocks of some particular chemical the crop-walker may be offered a financial incentive to push that chemical. In addition, each distributor does not carry every product on the market, so the products offered to farmers that rely on distributors are limited.[23]

By contrast, farmers that employ Independents are offered more sophisticated advice than that given to small farmers by distributors. The advice of Independents includes not only agrochemical solutions to problems, but remedies in rotation patterns, tillage, and natural resistance of seed varieties. Farmers that use Independents often reduce agrochemical usage through the use of these alternative solutions in order to reduce overall costs. According to Miles Thomas at the Central Science Laboratory (CSL): "Large farms are more aware of correct pesticide use and are more keen to cut rates if it will save them money. They are more inclined to experiment with reduced rates and cut rates to the limit to cut costs. So you'll find the most advanced experiments on the large farms. Small farmers don't have the time to experiment. They buy the product and apply as per directions. So the small farmer probably only goes in once at the recommended rate, whereas the larger farmer probably goes in at a lower rate and then perhaps has to go in again."[24]

As the person responsible for conducting national Pesticide Usage Surveys and collecting and disseminating data, Thomas is one of the most knowledgeable people about agrochemical use in the U.K. He has also found that the generally better-educated farmers who manage large farms are inclined to condition their agrochemical use on the variety of a crop receiving treatment. That is, if there are several varieties of a single crop on the farm, they will spray the more resistant varieties less often than they do the less resistant varieties. By contrast, the farmer of a small farm is more likely to treat all varieties the same. Thomas posits that the small farmer simply has less time to engage in differential treatment.

Thomas's expectations were confirmed during an interview with Philip Chamberlain, a farmer whose family has farmed a large amount of acreage for more than one hundred years. Chamberlain has found that he can reduce agrochemical use 25–75 percent from manufacturers' recommendations through the use of better equipment like air-assisted sprayers and multiple applications. On average, he has been able to reduce his use of agrochemicals to 60 percent of the recommended rates. Reducing usage rates from manufacturers' recommendations is possible in part because recommended rates are based on efficacy under the worst possible conditions.[25] Consequently, lower dosage rates can provide the same protection under normal or good conditions. Evaluating conditions to estimate the most efficient rates is, however, dependent on good information and comprehensive farmer education.

Farmer Education

As indicated above, the British extension service ADAS began charging farmers for agricultural advice in the mid-1980s. Given the need for farmers to engage in more environmentally sensitive farming methods, and the dominant role chemical distributors play in plant protection advice, some argue that free and independent advice was needed as much in the mid-1980s as it was after the war.[26] In fact, every group interviewed lamented the lack of free farmer education and placed most of the blame for environmental problems on those who do not use chemicals properly.[27]

In response to its critics, MAFF argues that the Farming Advisory and Wildlife Group (FAWG), a network of farm advisors formed by the Royal Society for the Protection of Birds more than twenty years ago and partially funded by government, provides exactly this type of "public good" advice.

There are, however, at least four reasons to believe that the government's faith in FWAG is misplaced. First, while FWAG's advice is not expensive, it is not free. Second, farmers must seek out its advice largely for environmental reasons, not economic. Thus, it is not the average farmer but only those most interested in new techniques and environmental responsibility who seek FWAG's advice and benefit from the program.[28] Third, FWAG's efficacy is severely limited by insufficient national resources and the requirement that it rely on concurrent, voluntary local funding. Finally, the actual number of available FWAG advisors precludes new contacts with more than 1–2 percent of British farmers each year.[29] If these real problems were not enough, many farmers do not have a positive opinion of FWAG because they see it as too "green" and on the "wrong side" of property rights issues.[30]

Training and Machine Certification

According to Winter, "If the advice situation is serious that of training is even worse. The ATB [Agricultural Training Board] Landbase survey revealed that only 3 percent of farmers had undertaken any environmental training in the previous five years. . . . Out of nearly 250,000 farmers in the U.K. just a few hundred seem to avail themselves of agri-environmental training provision each year" (1996:246).

Pesticide application requires certification only for those farmers born after 1964. Given the aging of the farm population, this grandfathers in a very large percentage of British farmers active during the study period. More important, certification requires little more than demonstration that a farmer can mix pesticides according to directions.[31] Thomas believes that many of the problems resulting from agrochemical use are due to bad equipment (1999). Unfortunately, nobody actually knows the state of farm machinery in the U.K. because that information is simply not collected. Theoretically, the training that leads to certification should teach those who spray pesticides to calibrate their equipment. Yet there is no legal framework to make sure the equipment is in good working order. "I think that is where we fall down at the moment in legislation in this country . . . spraying is very seasonal thing, farmers don't use the equipment for months on end and then they are out there from dawn to dusk during windows of opportunity" (Thomas 1999).

Supermarket and Miller Protocols

A second uniquely British variable to consider is supermarket protocols. Protocols are the rules farmers must follow in producing a crop for the supermarket to contract for its purchase. The evolution of supermarkets as the primary food suppliers traditionally contributed to high agrochemical use. For a supermarket, profit margins on produce far exceed those on other grocery items, and the appearance of fresh fruits and vegetables is paramount to those sales. If a farmer's crop has cosmetic flaws caused by insects, the farmer cannot sell to the retail stores and the crop is a loss. Given the untenability of such a loss, farmers historically used more pesticides than crop protection demands for the health of plants or for yields simply to meet appearance standards.[32] For first-stage food processors (especially canning), the appearance of a crop is less important, but the absence of insects is essential. Thus, both of the farmers' markets traditionally demanded agricultural products free of insects, regardless of necessity for health or impact on the environment.

The situation has changed dramatically. Supermarkets are now perceived to be the greatest force for more ecological farming in the U.K. Supermarkets have developed protocols governing agrochemical use in fresh fruit and vegetable production that farmers must follow to sell their products to the large chains. Consumer preferences drove the creation of supermarket protocols and testify to the fact that the British public is concerned about the public health effects of agrochemical use. Thus, it cannot be said that the British government has failed to constrain agrochemical use due to an absence of public demand. On the contrary, public support for clean agriculture is strong and consistent with public preferences on environmental issues generally. According to a leading scholar of environmental politics in Europe, "Britain has the oldest, strongest, best organized and most widely supported environmental lobby in the world" (McCormick 1991:34).

Protocols for fruits and vegetables have so impacted farmers' choices that the NFU, interested farmers, and large millers chose to develop their own protocol for arable crops to preempt new supermarket protocols. As the supermarkets' motive for limiting agrochemical use is not strictly environmental concern, but rather market position, retailers had not initially restricted agrochemical use on crops subject to processing. With the development of genetically modified organisms, however, even crops that are processed before they reach the consumer have become subject to public scrutiny. Therefore, the major millers in Britain have decided that they will not accept crops that are not grown according to protocol. As a result, like the produce farmers before them, arable farmers will have no choice but to follow the protocol if they want to continue farming.[33]

Free-marketers might argue that supermarket protocols are evidence that the market is working and there is no need for government regulation or taxpayer-funded programs. Environmentalists are, however, uncomfortable with the supermarkets playing that role because their motivation is not environmental protection, and supermarkets are not responsible for the protection of the environment.[34] Supermarket protocols are merely marketing techniques employed competitively to increase market share. Therefore, where the public is unaware of an environmental problem there is no reason for the retailers to institute change. Moreover, these protocols are largely in response to immediate and visible concerns and not to concerns regarding long-term water quality, wildlife issues, or an array of other variables that are the legitimate purview of ministries of agriculture, environment, and health. At best these protocols can respond to known health dangers. At worst they can create a false sense of security or even encourage practices that are not in the interest of the public or farmers.

Conclusion

The statistical evidence had already shown that trends in agrochemical use in the U.K. were much higher than in countries using PR. The question that motivated this case study was whether we could reasonably attribute the increase in agrochemical use over the past twenty-five years to government policy, or to the absence thereof. The answer is now clear: British governments have not enacted policies that impose concentrated costs on farmers or agrochemical manufacturers. While trends in agrochemical use in the U.K. increased relative to most other European countries, British governments did very little to reduce the use of fertilizers and pesticides, and what little was done was driven by EU directives. Moreover, the policies that were enacted to protect the environment relied entirely on the voluntary participation of farmers. Finally, in its tacit reliance on distributors for agrochemical advice, the government has either sanctioned the liberal use of fertilizers and pesticides, or ignored the fact that the status quo provides incentives for farmers, agrochemical manufacturers, and distributors to maximize agrochemical use.

Two alternative explanations for British policy—or the lack thereof—merit discussion. The first, public opinion, was touched on above. We expect that SMD competition and single-party majority governments like those in Britain to enact policies that are consistent with public preferences because voters can readily "throw the rascals out" if they do not. It is therefore important to note how much at odds public preferences are with British policy. As revealed in this case study, consumers' preferences for greener agricultural methods are so strong and so broad that supermarkets have created protocols that require farmers to limit agrochemical use on fruits and vegetables in response. This finding is consistent with the quantitative analyses in previous chapters that control for public opinion and find that it does not explain variance in agrochemical use. Britain is among the worst performers in agrochemical usage—and is considered an environmental laggard generally—yet 90 percent of the public reported being willing to support government action to protect the environment in the surveys conducted in the 1980s.[35]

It is also important to note that British citizens appear to be as environmentally conscious as citizens in some of the most "environmental" countries in the world. In fact, British voters self-report as being more willing to vote for a Green Party candidate if the electoral system allowed one any chance of winning than voters in Germany actually did when the Green Party entered government.[36] While self-reported intentions under a hypothetical situation (proportional representation) may be suspect, 15 percent of British voters did in fact vote for the Green Party in the 1989 elections to the European Parliament, despite the fact that the electoral system used at that time was first-past-the-post. This was the highest percentage of the national vote ever won by a Green Party in *any* European country. The Green Party actually polled 20 percent in some districts—second only to the conservatives.[37] Membership in environmental organizations also testifies to citizens' environmental preferences. In the late 1980s Greenpeace's membership stood at almost 300,000, Friends of the Earth membership at 125,000.[38]

The alternative explanation identified in the introduction to this book is that it is not the British system but the conservative ideology of the party that governed Britain for twenty of the twenty-five years studied. As discussed in previous chapters, SMD elections tend to empower conservative governments and therefore it is often the case that policy outcomes driven by ideology and political institutions are observationally equivalent. The institutional argument made here is that the linkages between the NFU and the government would remain the same under any government and therefore policy choices are no more likely to impose costs under Labour than they do under the Tories.

Locating interest group power in the system rather than the governing party is supported by two facts in this case. First, British Conservatives under Margaret Thatcher were not anti-environment. Conservatives have historically been associated with conservation of the countryside, the primary environmental concern in Britain.[39] And it was Thatcher who eloquently made the case for conservation and environmental responsibility in an influential 1988 speech that generated significant media and public concern for the environment. According to Rootes, the effect was "dramatically to heighten the prominence of environmental issues and to give unprecedented respectability to their articulation" (1995:70). Finally, according to a 1989 opinion survey, most of the support for the Green Party in British election to the European Parliament came from supporters of the Conservative Party (29 percent), not Labour (18 percent).[40]

Second, the British Labour Party has shared the progrowth agenda of its conservative rivals, like many major parties of the left in countries dominated by two large parties. According to Rootes, environmental groups do not find Labour "hospitable" to their issues. He argues that Labour views the environmental movement as "selfish and middle class" and that Labour is only "green" when forced to be by Conservative and Liberal Democratic Parties (1995:84). Moreover, while the Labour government campaigns in part as the "greener" government; its policies do not bear out its rhetoric. After the Labour government came to power in 1997 it *eliminated* the NSA scheme, the only effective scheme to reduce agrochemical use in British history, on the grounds that it was too expensive. Furthermore, despite the continuing problems generated by agrochemical use and recent losses in the European Court of Justice, the Labour government has not enacted any additional policies in this area.

More general conclusions about the British government's willingness to impose concentrated costs for environmental protection can also be made. The British government's preference for remedial methods over preventive measures is in clear conflict with the two fundamental principles of European environmental policy: the Precautionary Principle and the Polluter Pays Principle. The British articulation of both principles is revealing. The Precautionary Principle states that where there are significant risks of damage to the environment the government is prepared to limit the use of dangerous materials. But the British articulation qualifies that statement, stating that "if the future costs are likely to be very high *and action now is relatively inexpensive,* or if irreversible effects are indicated, the Government is prepared to take action now" (emphasis added). British articulation of the Polluter Pays Principle is equally revealing. According to the U.K.'s Environmental Protection Act of 1990 (43), one of the guiding principles of environmental protection is "the best available techniques *not entailing excessive cost*" (BATNEEC). All other countries studied articulate a goal of the "best available technology" in principle, without qualification. These statements of principle therefore not only qualify the government's willingness to protect the environment, they institutionalize a cost-benefit calculation of the common interest that advantages existing economic concerns over future environmental quality.

6

GERMANY: THE POLITICS OF PAYING
THE POLLUTER

Germany was selected for in-depth study for three reasons. First, as a longtime member of the European Union, Germany was, like Britain, subject to the Common Agriculture Policy (CAP) during the study period.[1] Second, Germany's federal system provides variance on state organization, one of the independent variables argued to affect policy choice, especially in policy domains where interest groups are geographically concentrated. Third, and most important, Germany's mixed-member electoral system generates coalition governments typically containing one large party that shares power with a small party.[2] In contrast to the single-member district (SMD) elections that produced vulnerable single-party majority governments in Britain, the thesis anticipates that the proportional element of Germany's mixed system will produce multi-party governments and therein insulate politicians from interest group pressure to some degree.

As discussed in the theory chapter, expectations regarding the vulnerability of politicians elected in mixed-member systems are less straightforward than they are for politicians elected in either SMD or proportional representation (PR) alone. The thesis anticipates high vulnerability in political systems that use SMD to elect all representatives because the fate of individual politicians and the parties they represent can be decided by relatively few votes. Representatives elected in pure PR systems are expected to be less vulnerable to the demands of small groups because parties cannot only win seats with relatively few votes, they can remain in power even if they lose vote share. In mixed-member systems like that used in Germany, where politicians are elected in both SMD and PR races, both forces are at work. German voters are presented with a two-sided ballot, one side for the SMD race, one for the PR race. Voters cast one vote for an individual candidate to serve as the sole representative of the district in the SMD race, and a second vote for a party that will win seats in proportion to its total vote share in the multi-member district race.

The vulnerability thesis anticipates that politicians' incentives to acquiesce to interest group demands will vary in mixed-member systems depending on the size of the party to which they belong. The two large parties who compete in SMDs will be anxious to keep the support of small groups and will therefore be most vulnerable to the demands of interest groups that can tip the balance in SMD elections. The smaller parties who owe their seats to the PR portion of the ballot will, ironically, be less vulnerable to the demands of organized groups. Party leaders of all parties will, however, enjoy more insulation from interest group retribution than they would in SMD systems because the individuals most important to the party will be placed in safe positions at the top of party lists on the PR portion of ballots. Once the leaders of large parties are in government, the need to form coalitions and compromise with small parties will provide large parties with additional political cover from retribution for policy choice. Overall, therefore, mixed-member electoral systems should hinder both accountability and identifiability to provide politicians, especially the leaders of political parties, the insulation necessary to impose more concentrated costs on powerful groups than can their counterparts who lead single-party majority governments.

Importantly, however, we expect that Germany's federal structure will simultaneously inhibit the imposition of costs on powerful groups because subnational representatives can affect the design of national legislation or its implementation. The Bundesrat, the German legislative body that represents the *Länder* (states),[3] holds a veto on all legislation directly related to state responsibilities or any that must be implemented by the *Länder*. This equates to veto power over approximately 60 percent of national legislation.[4] In addition, the individual *Land* must normally enact subnational policies to provide the supporting legislation necessary to accomplish the goals of framework laws made at the national level. Consequently, politicians elected at the subnational level have the potential to be decisive over some national legislation, and they control the implementation of legislation once passed.

This case study explores the linkages between institutional design, policy choice, and environmental outcomes under these conditions. To facilitate comparison across states, this chapter will be structured as the previous one. The first section describes the agricultural situation in Germany and the major policies directed at agrochemicals enacted at the national level. The second section goes to the field to identify any unforeseen determinants of agrochemical use. The third section concludes, focusing attention on the role of federalism in policy choice and the politics of "paying the polluter."

Agriculture and the Environment in Germany

Six decades ago Germany's early policies toward agriculture were, like those of all European countries, driven by the need to increase production rapidly after World War II. Mechanization, specialization, and intensification generated increases in agrochemical use beginning in the 1950s and continued unabated until the 1992 CAP reforms that created programs for extensification.[5] Like farmers across Europe, Germany's farmers relied on financial support from the government and EU subsides for a large portion of their income, estimated at near 50 percent in the mid-1990s.[6]

While half of the land in Germany is devoted to agriculture, the chemical industry is more important to Germany's economy. The industry was responsible for 5 percent of Germany's GDP at the end of the study period, which was a larger percentage than any of the other nineteen countries studied, twice as high as the U.K., and three times that of Austria or Sweden. In addition, the German chemical industry employed approximately 8 percent of workers in the industrial sector and contributed 13 percent to total exports by 1990, which equaled more than 8 percent of the world's chemical sales and more than 17 percent the world's chemical exports.[7]

The environmental consequences of agrochemical use are also significant in Germany. According to the German government, "More than half of all nitrogen loads and over 40 percent of all phosphate loads to Germany's water resources originate from agricultural land. . . . Water production facilities have had to be closed down in virtually every region in Germany, especially in agricultural areas."[8] In addition, "Survey results from the *Länder* show that approximately ten percent of all measuring units in near-surface groundwater indicate concentrations of plant protection agents above the European Union's .1 g/l limit."[9] The costs to decontaminate the drinking water supply from fertilizers and pesticides "amounted to over DM 920 million at the end of the 1980's."[10]

Interest Groups and Policy Choice: The Role of Corporatism

Unlike Britain, the interest group system in Germany is formally corporatist. Hierarchically organized peak organizations representing labor, business—and farmers—enjoy a formal role in policy making.[11] While the interest group system generates significant differences in power relationships between labor and business, political relationships for farmers' groups do not differ much in pluralist and corporatist systems. As in Britain, the most important interest group representing German farmers, and one of the most powerful interest groups in Germany, is the German Farmers' Union, the DBV.[12] Established in 1948, the DBV is an umbrella organization of fifteen regional farm organizations and twenty-six other associated organizations that represented approximately 90 percent of Germany's farmers throughout the study period. Like the National Farmers Union in Britain, the power of the DBV is in its ability to speak with one clear voice for a very diverse group of farmers.

As in Britain, the Farmers' Union also enjoys a close relationship with policy makers. Complex personal contacts between the DBV, various ministries, and the government provide the DBV with direct influence on policy. The DBV president and the Minister of Agriculture meet regularly, and the president of the DBV usually seeks discussions with the Minister of Agriculture, the Ministry of Economics, and even the Foreign Office before important decisions are made. The DBV president may also request, and is usually granted, an interview with the German chancellor. There are similar networks of contacts at the *Länder* level as well.[13] "The farmers union is a very important player in policy making because they are important—nothing happens without the Union's OK."[14] Given our previous discussion of the European Union, it is also important to note that the DBV enjoys continuous access to EU decision makers through ministry officials.

Political Vulnerability, Party System Dynamics, and Policy Influence

Between 1970 and 1995, Germany's two large political parties, the Christian Democratic Union/Christian Social Union (CDU/CSU)[15] and the Social Democratic Party (SPD), alternated in government with the Free Democratic Party (FDP), a small party capturing approximately 10 percent of the vote. The CDU/CSU and SPD both won large minorities of the vote, but both needed additional support to command a parliamentary majority.[16]

It is widely believed that the structure of the party system enhances farmers' political power in Germany. Farmers have historically been represented by the CDU/CSU, yet they also wield significant power through the smaller FDP. While the FDP is a very small party, it has played a pivotal role in German government formation because it traditionally controlled enough seats to give either of the two large parties a majority. Importantly for policy making affecting agrochemicals, the SPD governed in coalition with the FDP whenever the CDU/CSU was out of power during the study period, and its pivotal position allowed the FDP to control important ministries, including the Ministry of Agriculture.[17]

Although the percentage of farmers voting for the FDP is small, the farm vote is often a large percentage of the party's total vote. The relative importance of the farm vote for the FDP is important because the German electoral system requires that a party receive a minimum of 5 percent of the vote in order to claim its proportion of seats in parliament. Therefore, the FDP cannot afford to lose its farm vote because it relies almost entirely on the PR portion of the vote to meet the 5-percent threshold. In addition, the electoral system allows farmers to be very influential in *Länder* elections in crucial states. According to scholars of agricultural policy in Europe, "German farmers have been able to extract such favors as a result of their position as swing voters in critical electoral regions of the liberal Free Democrats in Bavaria and for the Christian Democrats in north Germany. Such strength has been supplemented by the unity of the German farmers' union, the DBV" (Ockenden and Franklin 1995:28–29).

Policies Affecting the Use of Agrochemicals

In contrast to the near total dominance of voluntary agreements in the U.K., German policy is replete with formal "command and control" legislation at the national and *Land* level. The national government generally makes framework legislation that sets down broad policy outlines and oftentimes quantifiable standards, but leaves the enactment of more detailed law to the individual *Länder.* Within the environmental arena, national standards are typically set regarding the maximum level of pollutants to ensure uniformity across states. The *Länder* often enact additional legislation to achieve outcomes that meet national standards, and they are responsible for enforcing all federal legislation. This results in a fragmented policy environment that includes national and subnational legislation in most policy areas.

PESTICIDE REGULATION The fragmentation is evident in the plethora of regulations affecting the use of pesticides. The earliest legislation governing pesticides in Germany was the 1968 Pesticide Act, amended in 1986 by the Plant Protection Act, which governed the registration of pesticides through the 1990s.[18] Other national regulations governing pesticides include the 1972 Act on DDT, the Toxic Substances Control Act of 1980 (also known as the Chemicals Act), the Act Governing the Marketing and Use of Plant Protection Products of 1993, the Act Governing the Amendment of Plant Protection and Seed Regulations of 1993, and the Federal Water Act. Ordinances are also used to supplement framework legislation. Relevant ordinances include the Ordinance on Bans and Restrictions on Plant Protection Products of 1987, the Ordinance Governing Specialist Qualification in Plant Protection of 1987, the Plant Inspection Ordinance of 1989, and the Ordinance Governing the Protection of Bees from Hazards Caused by Plant Protection Products of 1992.[19] Ordinances limit the use of pesticides during certain periods, ban the use of certain products in specific areas, and require pesticide users to be licensed and machines used for pesticide application to be checked every two years.[20]

The Federal Biological Research Centre for Agriculture and Forestry (BBA), a research and administrative organization attached to the Federal Ministry of Consumer Protection, Food and Agriculture (BMVEL), is the agency responsible for pesticide registration. The BBA examines all products and registers only those that do not pose health or environmental threats when used properly. Permits are not granted if model calculations and lysimeter investigations[21] indicate that the EU limit of .1 g/l will be exceeded.[22] The BBA is also responsible for the testing of equipment used to spray pesticides, and it conducts its own field trials on all equipment authorized for sale in the country. In addition, the BBA "ascertains the fate of plant protection products and harmful chemical substances (i.e. heavy metals) in the environment; studies the effects that plant protection products have on organisms mainly in agricultural areas and near bordering waters (ecotoxicology); draws-up computerized benefit-risk-assessments for the application of plant protection products and investigates the possible effects of climatic changes on pests and plant protection strategies."[23]

Pesticide registration is valid for ten years and can be withdrawn by the BBA. The ten-year approval period is argued to force product evolution.[24] Ministers of Labor, Agriculture, and Health can also withdraw authorization by decree.[25] However, if the government decides to ban a product within its ten-year authorization period, the producer must be compensated for "breaking the contract."[26]

The BBA reports to the agriculture ministry, but it is also responsible to the environment agency for some environmental aspects, including those relating to agrochemical pollution. The Federal Environmental Agency has been an approval authority for plant protection agents since 1987. By law, the agriculture ministry must also consult with an expert body of appointed representatives of various interests.[27] Given the scope of Germany's regulatory environment, and the prominence of environmental concerns, it is interesting to recall that there are no regulations governing pesticides in the U.K., save two voluntary schemes that verified product efficacy and health risks to applicators; neither of which assessed the environmental impacts of pesticide use.

FERTILIZER REGULATIONS As in Britain, the major policies affecting fertilizer use have largely been in response to EU directives. Unlike the situation in Britain however, determination of the Nitrate Vulnerable Zones was not problematic; Germany deemed the entire country vulnerable. Yet Germany's incorporation of the EU's Nitrate Directive into national legislation was more than two years late due to a disagreement between the Ministry of Agriculture and the Ministry of Environment.[28] The timing of the implementing legislation renders it immaterial to the use of fertilizers during the study period, but the political process that forestalled the legislation during the period is enlightening theoretically and bears close examination here.

The disagreement between the ministries concerned the wording of the requirement that farmers use only as much fertilizer as dictated by plant "needs." The dispute was over the determination of those needs, specifically whether or not the nutrients already available in the soil should be counted toward fulfilling plant needs. The initial proposal dictated that where the soil is rich in nutrients, fertilizer use should be reduced accordingly. Water suppliers had gone to environmental ministries of the individual *Land* governments in support of the proposal, arguing that there was no need to use additional fertilizer on already rich soil. The farmers' union was strongly against the proposal, arguing that this requirement would hurt farmers because they would have "excess" manure that they would then have to store. In a battle to stop the proposal, the DBV calculated the number of farms that might fail if the law went through and initiated letter writing campaigns from regional unions to *Land* governments. Farmers across the country demanded that they be allowed to fertilize according to "current plant needs." The DBV was successful in its campaign, and farmers won the legal right to ignore nutrients available in the soil when calculating plant needs without violating the law.[29]

The Ordinance on the Principles of Good Professional Practice in the Field of Fertilisation, a.k.a. The Ordinance on Fertilisation, was finally adopted on January 26, 1996. While the ordinance allowed farmers to ignore soil quality in calculating plant needs, it did impose some significant costs. Those who farm more than ten hectares must calculate nitrogen surpluses annually, and phosphorus and potassium every three years. Calculations must include the application of organic, inorganic, and sludge fertilizers (from urban sewage treatment), crops that fix nitrogen, and the withdrawal of nitrogen with the harvest. Changes in crops must also be taken into consideration, and records must be kept for nine years.[30] As a result, the process forces farmers to become aware of how much excess fertilizer they are using. The ordinance also regulated farm machinery, requiring that equipment ensure appropriate application rates and distribution as well as low-loss application. The ordinance also allows authorities to issue instruction on compliance and determine buffers, i.e., minimum distances from surface water bodies, and it prohibits application of fertilizers to saturated, frozen, or snow covered land.[31]

Citing "competitive disadvantages," the DBV has since criticized the ordinance for regulating phosphorus and potassium.[32] The DBV has also won a softening on the conditions under which manure may be applied to land in the winter, restricting application to "deeply" frozen soil or land covered in a "heavy" snow.[33] Importantly, however, the mere act of calculating nutrient balances, even if a farmer may disregard them, appears to have had a significant impact on farmers' behavior. According to Eichler and Schultz, "One of the main effects of the ordinance on fertilizing is a widespread discussion between farmers and extension services on bookkeeping of nutrients and—as a consequence—efficient nutrient management including fertilization. Thus scientific results and knowledge are integrated faster into farmers' performance which leads to a higher efficiency and less environmental pollution by nutrient losses."[34]

In total, therefore, and especially by comparison to the British case, German legislation imposes multiple costs on farmers, despite the fact that at least one party in government relied heavily on the farm vote and despite the formal policy-making power and heavy political influence of the DBV. While the DBV won concessions that minimized immediate costs, most farmers must still spend significant time and energy satisfying the ordinance. What is interesting about the history of fertilizer policy is that the DBV orchestrated a campaign focused at regional, rather than national level, policy makers to affect the design of national legislation. This is consistent with the theoretical expectations regarding the role of federalism in inhibiting cost imposition. Notably, however, the national coalition government was still able to impose costs on farmers and indirectly on fertilizer manufacturers, which is also consistent with theoretical expectations.

EU AGRI-ENVIRONMENTAL MEASURES The agri-environmental measures created with the 1992 CAP reform have been utilized by some subnational authorities to provide funding to farmers that ultimately helps protect the environment. "Germany has more agri-environmental

schemes . . . in place than any other EU Member State. Almost all have
been introduced by the *Länder* authorities. . . . [A]t the end of 1992 there
were 104 schemes available to farmers in Germany, 91 of which ostensibly
had environmental protection as the main or shared objective."[35] By the
end of the study period, 29 percent of the total utilized agricultural area
was under voluntary agri-environmental schemes.[36]

The impact of these measures on environmental quality is, however,
subject to debate. Some researchers argue that the same methods would
likely be chosen in the absence of the schemes. They find little or no reduction in livestock numbers, no changes in current farming practices, and no
conversion to organic production.[37] Others dispute that assessment, at least
as it pertains to subsidies for organic production. According to statistics
kept by the Federal Environmental Agency, while organic farming grew
steadily during the 1980s it increased dramatically in the 1990s in large part
due to support programs. By the end of the study period, organic production accounted for approximately 2 percent of the total agricultural area.[38]

The Determinants of Agrochemical Use

National legislation is clearly an important determinant of farmers'
use of pesticide and fertilizers. Much of the legislation designed to reduce
pollution from fertilizers and pesticides is, however, "framework" legislation
that mandates outcomes, not methods. As in other policy areas, national
policy is articulated, implemented, and enforced at the *Land* level. The fact
that federal regulations must be implemented by the *Länder* has two consequences. First, it allows the Bundesrat, the upper house of the legislature,
formal veto authority over national policy. Second, it delegates responsibility for achieving policy goals to the *Länder*. This allows significant
policy variance between states because each *Land* government is entitled
to choose different methods to achieve national goals. The devolution of
power to the subnational level is important in two areas: farmer education
and water management.

Agricultural Chambers and Farmer Education

The individual *Land* are responsible for all farmer education. In
most of the *Länder*, the agricultural chambers fulfill this obligation. All

farmers must be members of their local agriculture chamber, and they pay a membership fee based on their land value that entitles them to chamber services. Chambers are financed jointly by farmers and the *Länder*, with the Agriculture Ministry funding approximately 60 percent of the chambers' activities, farmers' fees funding the remaining 40 percent. The people who work in the chambers are civil servants, but the president of the chamber is a farmer. While the chambers must fulfill some government requirements, e.g., policing certification, farmers decide what activities the chambers undertake. In *Länder* without agriculture chambers, e.g., in Bavaria, East Germany, and Frankfurt, the government provides a similar set of services.[39]

One of the most important functions of the agriculture chambers is to provide farmers with information about pesticides and fertilizers. Chambers provide most of the information a farmer receives, including information on pest infestations, the efficacy of agrochemicals at different dose rates, and the results of the chambers' independent field trials.[40] It is therefore important to note that the national Plant Protection Law of 1986 mandates that chamber advice go beyond providing information on chemicals, to include teaching alternative or nonchemical methods of pest control. Often the agriculture chamber will get a new pesticide before it is registered, in which case the chamber receives funding to check the claims of the manufacturer. Chambers also do field trials on farmers' fields in exchange for advice. Field trials are partially funded by manufacturers because the trial is considered a service for the manufacturer, but the chambers use their own sprayers to control dose, they control the time of application, and they test the mode of action and efficacy.

Tellingly, most of the field trials are at *half* the manufacturers' recommended rate. Some chambers use as little as 20–30 percent dose rates because they have found not only that the lower rates are efficacious, but that lower rates also minimize resistance problems. Information about the efficacy of reduced rates is passed on to farmers through the regular course of advice, i.e., through newsletters and by phone. However, product labels are *not* changed to reflect the efficacy of reduced dose rates, or the conditions under which lower doses are most efficacious.[41] Nevertheless, well-educated farmers using good equipment normally apply 30–50 percent of the manufacturer's recommended dose rate because information from the chambers allows them to apply chemicals judiciously, at the right time and under the right conditions.[42]

The chambers also enforce government policy. They pay independent contractors to inspect suppliers of pesticides to verify that they do not sell nonregistered products; they police farmers in water-sensitive areas and train those who certify sprayers. Every two years sprayers must be rechecked and farmers must display labels that verify inspection.[43] According to representatives of the chamber in Hannover, national policies that mandate that the chambers consider the environment have made a substantial difference in chamber activities. For example, as a product of the 1996 Ordinance on Fertilizers, the agriculture chambers were charged with producing fertilizer recommendations. Recommendations were determined by taking soil samples and running field trials. Farmers had to pay DM 25 per soil layer, and needed one sample for every ten hectares to test the nitrogen level, and one sample for every two to three hectares to test phosphorus and potassium levels. The Hannover chamber found that farmers were using close to the recommended amount of nitrogen, but up to 20 percent more phosphorus and potassium than the agriculture chamber would recommend.[44]

Paying the Polluter: Drinking Water Supplier–Farmer Co-ops

Reductions in the use of agrochemicals are also a product of agreements between water suppliers and farmers. Water suppliers contract with farmers in sensitive areas to reduce or eliminate their use of agrochemicals to protect water supplies. These are not voluntary schemes like those in Britain where farmers in designated areas can choose to participate. These contracts are motivated by the Federal Water Act (1986), which allows for the designation of "Water Protection Areas" (WPAs) wherein the government may limit the use of agrochemicals and compensate affected farmers for doing so. The Federal Water Act is framework legislation and therefore requires the *Länder* to enact specific laws to accomplish the act's more general ends. Since the design of policies and their implementation is left to the *Länder*, the nature of the policies can and does differ between states.

There are two basic approaches to the financing of compensatory payments.[45] One approach, adopted by Baden-Württemberg, requires water treatment plants to pay a tax to the state government on the water they use. That tax then funds compensatory payments to farmers in the WPAs who are restricted in their use of agrochemicals.[46] The regulation limits the use of nitrogen fertilizer to 80 percent of the usual rate. If soil samples after the harvest register more than 45 kg/ha of nitrogen, it is assumed that the farmer has not complied with the regulation. In nine of the sixteen *Länder* in Germany, water is taxed to fund compensatory payments.[47]

A second approach is used in North Rine-Westphalia. In that approach the government's role is limited to supporting the cooperation between water treatment plants and farmers. Both parties are required to negotiate agreements over farming methods and the use of agrochemicals. Compensatory payments are paid to the farmers directly by the water treatment plants that benefit from the restrictions.

In addition to paying farmers not to use certain chemicals, water supply companies also pay for additional extension services for farmers.[48] During an interview in 1999, a representative of a water supplier described the process by which his organization works with farmers to minimize leaching.[49] The water supplier first conducted soil samples to a depth of 90 cm for nitrogen and ammonia to estimate the likely deficiency or surplus based on crop needs. Data collected informed the precrop analysis, which in consideration of other factors ultimately generated the recommended fertilization rate. Extension service workers employed by the water supplier advised farmers on methods to accomplish this rate and on specific methods to reduce leaching, including the use of cover crops and low tillage techniques. Farmers were free to choose which methods to use, but the water supplier resampled the soil after harvest to verify that the farmer had in fact reduced leaching. The water supplier paid farmers 140 Deutsche Marks (DM) per hectare to engage in the behaviors deemed necessary to preclude water contamination. In addition, farmers received additional services and products that included seeds and pesticides to ensure success. Co-ops cost the water supplier approximately 450,000 DM/year for groundwater and .009 DM/m3 of drinking water.

Many argue that co-ops have been very successful, especially with nitrogen control. In the words of one Agriculture Ministry official, "After 12 years, Paragraph 19/4 of the Federal Water Act doesn't follow the 'Polluter Pays Principle,' but it works."[50] In fact, co-ops became so successful that by the end of the study period there were an estimated 150 co-ops in Germany.[51] The ability of farmers in WPAs to reduce agrochemical use *without* affecting yields also caught the attention of farmers not involved in the co-ops. The resulting transfer of technology and education outside of the WPAs helped to increase environmental awareness and reduce agrochemical use throughout Germany.[52]

Where water supplier co-ops do not exist, there are state-run programs to reduce nitrogen use by 20 percent in areas that affect groundwater. Farmers are compensated per hectare, and nitrogen levels are tested after harvest to verify that farmers have taken necessary actions. While the yields in those areas were slightly reduced, they have not gone down as much as anticipated so compensation exceeded losses.[53] According to an Agriculture Ministry official however, regulated areas are less successful than areas under co-op agreements. In explaining their success, Lübbe argued that co-ops have been successful because "both sides sit together and discuss problems" (1999).

Conclusion

As anticipated by the vulnerability thesis, coalition governments enacted a plethora of laws to reduce agrochemical use, but *Länder* authorities effectively transferred the costs of those policies from the minority who created the pollution to the public at large. More important theoretically, parties within national coalition governments were able to impose significant costs on critical constituencies. Therefore, contrary to theories that locate public good provision in the aggregation of minority interests, coalition governments in this case study were able to produce public goods because policy makers imposed necessary costs on their own constituencies.

The case study also demonstrates that where subnational politicians have power over national legislation they will strive to inhibit geographically concentrated costs. Clearly, the veto power of the Bundesrat empowered regionally strong farmers with disproportionate influence in the making of the Ordinance on Fertilizers. It is also clear that locating responsibility for the implementation of national policy at the *Länder* level facilitated the transfer of costs from a small group of polluters to the larger (water consuming) public. Ambitious framework legislation at the national level notwithstanding, the avoidance of cost imposition defined the *Land*-level response to agricultural pollution. Given Germany's "green" credentials, its reputation as an environmental leader, and its vocal commitment to the Polluter Pays Principle in rhetoric, its use of instruments that "pay the polluter" deserves further attention.

Paying the Polluter

While paying farmers to reduce agrochemical pollution contradicts the Polluter Pays Principle, it does offer several important advantages. First, it works. Paying the polluter encourages a rapid shift in the behavior of polluters, achieving environmental protection faster than can be accomplished by many alternative policies, however more "principled" in theory. Where the primary goal is environmental protection, policies should arguably be evaluated on their ability to achieve that end efficiently. Second, subsidizing environmental protection is politically painless—polluters do not rally against payments for environmental goods. Given that the political and economic power of polluters is often a major obstacle to environmental protection, the tenability of policy choice is a serious consideration. Third, behavioral changes have contagion effects. As reported above, when farmers reduced their reliance on agrochemicals without reducing yields, farmers outside the most sensitive areas also changed their behavior. Finally, farmers who participated in the programs changed their beliefs about the need to use label rates because they knew firsthand that lower doses were equally effective. As a result, the educational effects of altered behavior outlast particular programs.

The final reason that paying the polluter is often smart policy is simply that it is economically efficient compared with maintenance of the status quo. The economic and ecosystem costs of continued pollution, not to mention the costs imposed on taxpayers to formulate, implement, and enforce command and control legislation, should not be discounted. An example from this policy area illustrates. In a study done using the "Regionalised Agricultural and Environmental Information System" (RAUMIS), a model designed for quantitative analyses of agricultural and environmental policy, researchers found that protecting water supplies from excess nitrogen was always cheaper in the long run than allowing their continued contamination. If the aim of policy was to protect all of groundwater, findings indicate that the most cost-efficient policy would impose taxes on nitrogen and uniform restrictions in exchange for compensatory payments on the whole of the country. If the goal of policy was to protect only drinking water supplies, researchers found that measures targeted at farmers in specific areas would affect the desired outcome at the least cost. In the end, however, either uniform or targeted policies were welfare enhancing compared to the status quo use of fertilizers.[54]

It is notable that the RAUMIS study supports the use of agrochemical taxes as the most efficient method of altering farmers' behavior. Taxes impose the most obvious costs and are for that reason unlikely to be used in systems vulnerable to interest group pressure. Given the relative vulnerability of the two large parties that alternate in power in the German system, it is not surprising that agrochemical charges were not used in Germany during the study period. Taxes were, however, used effectively in the two remaining countries selected for in-depth study, Austria and Sweden—both of which use party list PR electoral systems. Given Austria's similarities with Germany, the next chapter examines the Austrian case in depth to explore the role institutions played in the adoption of taxes and other chemical reduction measures.

7

AUSTRIA: POLITICAL COVER AND POLICY CHOICE

While significantly smaller than Germany, neighboring Austria shares a similar geography and culture, both interest group systems are corporatist, and both are federal. Those similarities serve as important natural controls that facilitate comparison on other aspects, the most important of which derive from the electoral system. Austria is an important case study because its use of pure proportional representation (PR) generated single-party majority government, a bare majority coalition government, and grand coalition government during the study period. The varied composition of Austrian governments between 1970 and 1995 provides an opportunity to examine the policies of different types of governments acting in the same institutional environment. It allows us to test the expectation that government type, normally a product of the electoral system, renders politicians differentially vulnerable to interest group pressure. A final consideration for comparative analysis is that Austria became a member of the EU only in 1995 and was not therefore subject to the EU's Common Agricultural Policy or environmental directives.

The chapter is divided into three sections corresponding with the structure of the preceding chapters. The first section describes the agricultural situation in Austria, emphasizing similarities and differences to the countries already discussed. It also describes the major policies affecting agrochemical use, highlighting for the first time the potential of agri-environmental-type schemes to have a substantial impact on farmers' behavior. The second section analyzes the determinants of use, once again finding that federalism is a potent force in policy design, especially evident when the structure of farming varies significantly by region. The third section concludes with a discussion of the role of government type in providing the political cover necessary for costly policy choice.

Agriculture and the Environment in Austria

Austrian farms are small by comparison to those in the U.K. and Germany, ranging in size from ten to thirty hectares. More important, however, is the fact that there are two distinct types of farms in Austria: larger farms in the northeast, where flatter land allows arable cropping, and the smaller farms in the mountainous center and northwest, which are generally engaged in dairy and sheep production. This difference is critical to understanding both politics and policy in the Austrian federal system.

Interest Groups and Policy Choice

Like German policy making, Austria's corporatist system of interest group representation fosters formal and close connections between the Ministry of Agriculture and the Agriculture Chamber. As in Germany, the Agricultural Chamber is a peak organization, composed of nine provincial chambers that correspond to the nine *Länder*. And like the farmers' union in Germany, the head of the farmers' chamber is included in all decisions that affect farmers.[1] While the Ministry of Agriculture normally discusses issues with many groups, including the Ministry of the Environment and nongovernmental organizations like the World Wildlife Fund, the most important players are the nine *Land*-based agricultural chambers (PRAKO). If the chambers do not accept a policy proposal, it will not become law.[2] In addition, every political party has within it a farmers' organization, and all chambers are very close to political parties, especially the conservative People's Party, the ÖVP.[3] The leaders of the nine provincial chambers are often party leaders as well, and therefore the same people may fill government, party, and chamber positions, just as they do in Germany.[4]

Policies Affecting Agrochemical Use

While the decision-making process resembles that of Germany, the policies chosen do not. There are two significant differences. First, Austrian governments subsidized particular *methods* of production, rather than the amount of production.[5] In fact, prior to 1995, Austria's strong and varied support of "ecological farming," i.e., farming methods designed to minimize environmental damage, was the defining characteristic of Austrian agricultural policy. A substantial number of additional subsidies were paid on a per farm basis as well. As a result, as much as one-third of farmers' incomes came from "direct payments" for the practice of specific agricultural methods, regardless of production.[6] The second significant difference is as indicated in the conclusion of the previous chapter, the fact that Austrian governments used economic instruments (primarily taxes) to reduce the use of fertilizers.

SUBSIDIES FOR ENVIRONMENTALLY FRIENDLY FARMING METHODS   As the German case study made clear, "paying the polluter" can be an especially efficacious policy approach because subsidies work quickly and they often engender learning experiences that change farmers' behavior permanently. The attitude of farmers toward agrochemicals is an extremely important consideration in policy choice. The idea that unseen chemicals may harm the environment at some point in the distant future and oftentimes at a distant place has been difficult for many farmers to accept. As indicated in British case study, many farmers are especially reluctant to believe that controls on nitrogen are necessary. While pesticides are more readily accepted as potentially dangerous, farmers generally believe that the benefits of pesticide use outweigh the dangers. Government provision of subsidies that support more environmentally benign farming methods can shift farmers' perception of environmental risk because economic subsidies demonstrate the state's value of the environment and testify to the polluting potential of conventional agriculture.

Given that the benefits of reduced agrochemical use benefit distant publics, in time and space, it is not surprising that the impetus for ecological farming subsidies came from outside of the Agriculture Ministry. The first decrees aimed at organic farming were made in 1983 by the Ministry of Consumer Protection (then a part of the Ministry of Health).[7] The approach that would structure Austria's future policies was, however, the brainchild of Federal Minister of Agriculture Josef Riegler. His 1986 decision to break from the common perception of organic farming as outside mainstream agriculture, and reorient policy to make organic farming attractive to as many farmers as possible, put Austria on a path far different from other European countries. Riegler defended the shift in policy as the most effective route to achieving a number of agricultural goals simultaneously: i.e., reduce the use of agrochemicals, reduce commodity surpluses, support the farming sector, and respond to consumer demands for environmental goods.[8]

Change began almost immediately. Environmental objectives became part of the 1988 Farm Act and in 1989 funds for environmentally benign agriculture were reserved in the general budget for the first time.[9] Nearly 2.5 million Austrian shillings (ATS) were used to support the development of organic farmers' associations.[10] That initial investment in organizational infrastructure has since been described as indispensable to the growth of organic farming in Austria.[11] One year later, the Ministry of Agriculture started to support organic farmers from its own resources.[12]

The Agriculture Ministry initially pursued a "market niche model" strategy. Anticipating that farmers would be able to command high prices once they were able to sell products as "organic," subsidies were initially intended to support farmers during the transitional period from conventional to organic production. Many believed that the obstacle to organic farming was not the profitability of organic production, but the fact that the investment required to shift from conventional to fully organic production in one step was too expensive for most farmers. Policy emphasis was therefore on "middle level" programs that paid farmers to engage in certain specific methods that were components of organic production, but not fully organic.[13]

It soon became clear, however, that this niche strategy was not adequate to maintain large numbers of organic farms over the long term. A niche strategy dependant on high prices for organic products worked only for some products, and only for farmers close to markets in large cities. It was also argued that if the policies were effective and a large portion of agricultural land was eventually farmed organically, farmers would not be able to charge premium prices for what would become common techniques. If farmers could not charge higher prices for organic products, organic farmers would not be able to survive because organic farming is more expensive than conventional farming. Thus, if the government wanted to protect the environment through the maintenance of organic farms, it would have to compensate farmers for the provision of environmental goods *indefinitely*.[14]

Early awareness of the implications of a niche strategy allowed the government to anticipate future problems, and in 1992 Austria adopted a new "agri-environmental model" of subsidies to replace the market niche model.[15] In keeping with the original intent to make ecological farming accessible to as many farmers as possible, the new model was structured to support partially organic production methods permanently—not just "in transition." The Program for an Environmentally Sound Agriculture, known by its German acronym, ÖPUL, was created to channel subsidies to farmers for a variety of nonconventional practices that stopped short of fully organic production. Unlike programs in most other countries, the Austrian program was designed with a pyramid-like structure. At the lowest level, the Basis program provided elementary support, demanding few requirements so a large number of farmers could qualify. Higher up the pyramid, more ecologically beneficial methods of agriculture were supported individually, with organic production at the top.[16]

The plethora of individual subsidies available to farmers encouraged farmers to make small changes. Some subsidies supported farmers that engaged in certain crop rotations, others supported farmers who renounced the use of growth regulators. Separate subsidies supported farmers who reduced their use of commercial fertilizers or fungicides but otherwise practiced conventional farming. Special subsidies existed for the extensification of cereal production and livestock farming, which required greater land use for the same yield, in addition to subsidies for simple grassland management. Integrated vegetable, wine, or fruit production was also independently supported.[17] The multi-faceted approach is in stark contrast to the conventional methods of supporting only wholly organic production, which normally requires all these practices at the same time, and for an extended period of time, to ensure that all chemicals have been eliminated from the land.

The resulting pyramid of independent subsidies made some aspects of ecological farming accessible to the vast majority of farmers, and it allowed farmers to make the transition to organic farming incrementally, and without suffering the costs associated with lower yields, especially at the outset.[18] Programs also included per farm and per hectare payments, which compensated farmers for the difference in income compared to conventional farming.[19] The advantages of the program were numerous: markets were stabilized through the reduction of surpluses; individual subsidies generated a substantial reduction in agrochemical use; reductions in agrochemical use left soil, air, and water supplies in better condition; farmers' incomes were maintained; and the government used tax dollars to provide the environmental goods sought by society.[20]

In addition to direct payments, the state also supported the research necessary to further the development of organic farming. The federal government was very aware that the chambers that provide extension services must have trained personnel if they were to actively promote environmentally friendly agriculture.[21] The importance given education in the development of organic production was reflected in a ministerial address to an international conference on trade in organic farming. Agriculture minister Wilhelm Molterer stated that "the support of the market should not be confined to advertising measures, for the point is to bring about a change of attitudes of producers and consumers and this is only possible with intensive educational work" (1997:10).

FERTILIZER TAXES Austrian agricultural policy also differs from German and British policy in its use of taxes.[22] Taxes are difficult instruments to enact politically because they impose very visible costs on farmers and agrochemical manufacturers—groups already organized for economic reasons and therefore likely to act to preclude the imposition of costs. Yet as indicated in the previous chapter, many argue that taxing agrochemicals is the most efficient way to reduce agricultural pollution. Once a government has imposed a tax, it need not monitor compliance to ensure that farmers reduce their use of a chemical, or fund significant additional bureaucratic effort. Moreover, a tax encourages farmers to use agrochemicals judiciously, and judicious use can all but eliminate pollution.

Politicians, industry, and interest group representatives have argued, however, that taxes are inequitable because they punish those farmers who use agrochemicals efficiently along with those who do not. They point out that if agrochemicals are environmental pollutants only when they leach into water supplies, the efficient use of chemicals should not be taxed because it generates little if any leaching. Farmers' groups have also maintained that chemicals are expensive inputs and therefore farmers already optimize their use. For those reasons, some groups contend that agrochemical taxes hurt farmers and do little for the environment.

It is therefore notable that the Austrian government imposed taxes on nitrogen fertilizers in 1984 in order to reduce fertilizer consumption and relieve agricultural surpluses.[23] And, despite the claims of farmers' representatives, the fertilizer tax was credited with a 20 percent reduction in the use of chemical fertilizers between 1986 and 1993.[24]

The Determinants of Agrochemical Use

Interviewees across Austria identified government subsidies for ecological farming and fertilizer taxes as the main determinants of changes in agrochemical use during the study period. This fact differentiates Austria from both Germany and Britain, where nonstate actors had much more influence on farmers' behavior than policies enacted by elected politicians. The question is, how do we explain these policy choices?

Federalism and the Agriculture Chamber

The Agriculture Chamber was clearly the most influential designer of specific agricultural policies. Like Austria itself, the Agriculture Chamber is a federal organization that includes nine regional chambers and the farmers' credit organization. While the chamber is formally a peak organization wherein the leadership speaks for the member organizations, the importance of regional interests cannot be overstated. The organization of chambers is democratic, holding elections every three to five years, empowering the smaller, yet more numerous, mountain farmers.[25] However, the federal structure of the chamber ensures that the interests of farmers of both large arable farms and small mountain farms are represented.

The federal structure of agriculture chambers is the key to understanding the two-pronged approach that included both the imposition of fertilizer taxes and the creation of a unique program of subsidies for environmentally friendly farming. Recall that there are two distinct types of farms in Austria: large farms in the northeast, where flatter land allows mechanized farming methods, and small farms in the mountainous center and north-west that are unsuitable for mechanized production.[26] The small farmers in the mountainous areas profited the most from the ÖPUL program of ecological farming subsidies. These same small farmers also utilized manure for fertilizer so they were not greatly impacted by taxes on fertilizers. As indicated in the previous chapter, it is easy for governments to pay the polluter and therefore subsidies do not need more explanation.

Taxes, on the other hand, are politically difficult, and taxes on synthetic nitrogen fertilizers fell on farmers of larger arable farms in the northeast who did not benefit from environmental subsidies. These farmers use large quantities of fertilizer and were therefore initially opposed to fertilizer charges. However, these same farmers also use farm machinery that requires large quantities of fuel, and, unlike their counterparts in mountainous areas, they produce products that are primarily sold outside Austria. Consequently the Agriculture Chamber was able to orchestrate a deal that made fertilizer taxes palatable. Revenues from the fertilizer tax were returned to farmers through marketing programs, export subsidies, and rebates on diesel fuel. As farm machinery uses a significant amount of fuel, the rebate equated to substantial savings. In fact, export subsidies, marketing programs, and the lack of a diesel tax combined to create a net gain for farmers.[27]

The combination of policy instruments, subsidies for environmental farming, and compensated taxes on fertilizers offered benefits to all parties: farmers, the government, and consumers. Farmers of small mountain farms benefited from the creation of subsidies for ecological farming, while farmers of the larger arable farms benefited from rebated fertilizer taxes. Revenues from the fertilizer tax funded the export subsidies that helped government dispose of cereal surpluses that these farmers produced; a surplus that was becoming increasingly untenable with consumers, as it became increasingly expensive. Fertilizer taxes also helped to reduce chemical fertilizer use and, in combination with organic subsidies, provided consumers with environmental goods from agriculture.

Conclusion

While the power and the structure of the Chambers explain much of policy design, they do not explain the impetus behind specific policy goals, nor do they explain policy change. Organic farming had had a long tradition in Austria, beginning with the founding of the "biologic-dynamic" farms by the philosopher Rudolf Steiner between 1927 and 1935. In 1962 a second school of organic farming, called "organic-biologic," was created and established principles that dominate the sector even today.[28] Yet support for organic production did not increase gradually over time; it was instead a product of the single major policy shift discussed above. Interestingly, that policy shift was not experienced during the peak of environmentalism in the 1970s, but during a period of environmental retrenchment in the mid-1980s. This begs the question: Why did Austrian policy makers shift toward ecological farming when they did?

Party System Change and Government Type

Policy change closely mirrored party system change that affected government type. The Austrian party system has traditionally been dominated by two large parties, the Austrian People's Party (ÖVP) on the right and the Social Democratic Party (SPÖ) on the left. This outcome is quite unexpected because the electoral system is pure PR, which normally fosters a multi-party system wherein no single party wins a majority of the votes. Yet, between 1971 and 1983 the SPÖ did what very few parties are able to do in a PR system: it won a majority of the vote and governed alone in single-party majority governments. Given that these were the years of environmental awakening throughout the developed world, one might have expected a pro-environment shift during this period. Yet this was not the case. Majority support for the party of the left did not advantage environmental interests, despite the fact that the SPÖ had the power to enact its policy agenda.

Policy change began with party system change in 1983. In that year the SPÖ won a plurality of the vote but lost its majority status, and was forced to govern in coalition with the much smaller liberal Freedom Party FPÖ until 1986 as a result. The lack of government responsiveness to environmental concerns facilitated the continuing rise of the Green Party, which gained seats in the federal parliament for the first time in 1986. Its rise likely contributed to electoral losses for both the major parties that year, and arguably forced both large parties to become "greener," even against the wishes of their social partners.[29]

While some progress on environmental issues was made between 1983 and 1986, the most important initiatives in terms of environmental policy actually came when electoral losses forced the two large parties to govern together in a "grand coalition" from 1986 through 1995. Policy change was not, however, ideologically motivated. It was the newly nationalistic FPÖ that gained the most vote share in the 1986 election, suggesting that environmental issues were not the driving force behind party system change. Yet it was during this period that the two large parties were able to make a number of significant policy changes affecting the environment in several sectors, not just agriculture, and, importantly, against the wishes of the social partners.[30]

Political Cover and Policy Choice

As in any corporatist system, policy making in Austria is the joint responsibility of political parties and the peak organizations that represent business, labor, and farmers. According to Lauber, the monopolization of policy making by the two large parties and the corporatist "social partners" until the mid-1980s precluded environmental issues from gaining a political foothold because the ÖVP and the SPÖ allowed policy to be dominated by a progrowth agenda.[31] The Chamber of Commerce and the Agriculture Chamber, both of which are linked to the ÖVP, and the Chamber of Labor and the Trade Union Federation, which were linked to the SPÖ, are widely considered anti-environmental, presenting economic growth and environmental protection as antagonistic goals in public discussion.[32]

The vulnerability thesis predicts that governments will impose concentrated costs on powerful groups like these only when responsibility for decisions is obscured to preclude retribution by affected groups. The history of agricultural policy making in Austria is consistent with the theoretical expectations. Major policy change came only when the two major political parties were insulated from interest group retribution by entering a grand coalition, leaving interest groups with little political recourse to resist change.

It must be noted, however, that despite the fact that Austrian policies have imposed substantial costs that effectively protected the environment, farmers' representatives were able to bargain for economic benefits equal to or greater than the costs imposed. Federalism mattered to policy choice.

Environmental protection was used by subnational groups as a means to several unrelated ends. Subsidies were clearly a means to maintaining small-scale farming in low production areas and a rural population in areas that would, under free market conditions, struggle to survive. Just as clear, taxes on fertilizers were initiated to reduce surpluses, not to protect water supplies.

Nevertheless, taxes proved to be extremely valuable policy tools. Most important for the environment, they generated strong incentives to reduce waste quickly. The rebated tax encouraged all farmers to reduce their out-of-pocket expenses for fertilizers because actual use did not affect their gains from the rebate on fuel or export subsidies. Even before farmers were required to pay taxes on new supplies, they used existing stocks more judiciously to preclude future expenses. Economic instruments were also less expensive to administer than regulations used in other countries. If, like the Netherlands, the government chose to tax nutrient surpluses, an option that better targets polluters, high monitoring costs would likely have generated a net cost for taxpayers.[33] Finally, taxes force farmers to analyze their fertilizer consumption, in effect self-educating the farmer on the efficiency of his or her use and altering behavior accordingly. Behavioral "fixes" like these are arguably the most efficacious method of reducing pollution because they change attitudes that affect behavior far into the future.

The final case study, presented in the following chapter, serves as an interesting comparison to Austria in this respect. The Swedish government has imposed the most costs on farmers and agrochemical manufacturers of any of the governments studied. Sweden, like Austria, is also a corporatist system wherein farmers have a formal role in policy making. Yet, like the Austrian government, Swedish governments were able to impose significant costs on this well-represented group. Major differences between these two countries exist, however, because Sweden is a unitary state and because it has been governed by single-party minority governments or coalitions that depended on partisan cooperation to govern throughout the study period.

8

SWEDEN: MINORITY REPRESENTATION AND THE MAJORITY INTEREST

Like Austria, Sweden was not a member of the European Union during the study period. Also like Austria, Sweden is ranked among the most corporatist countries in the developed world,[1] and Swedish politicians are also empowered via a list-PR electoral system, the system argued to be most likely to limit interest group power. Unlike Austria, however, the organization of the Swedish state is unitary; Swedish governments do not share power with lower-level governments and should therefore be less vulnerable to regional interest group pressure. In fact, the institutional combination that defines the Swedish political system locates it at the far end of the vulnerability index, a ranking that anticipates the greatest government ability to impose concentrated costs for public goods.

The Social Democrats governed as a single-party minority government during most of the period under study, always in need of the support of one or more parties in parliament to pass legislation. When the Social Democrats were not in power, a coalition of nonsocialist parties governed together. At no time could any party pass legislation without the support of one or more other parties. This chapter will investigate the relationship between multi-party politics in a unitary system and government capacity to impose concentrated costs when necessary to achieve environmental goals.

As the others before it, this chapter is divided into three sections. The first section describes the agricultural situation in Sweden and the major policies affecting agrochemical use. The second section reports on field interviews where actors locate responsibility for outcomes explicitly in government decision-making institutions for the first time. The third section concludes with a focus on the core theoretical concern of this book, the relationship between multi-party decision making and government capacity to impose concentrated costs on its own constituencies.

Agriculture and the Environment in Sweden

Only 8 percent of Sweden's land area is under cultivation, and Sweden contributes comparatively little to agricultural production in Europe. Agriculture's average contribution to Sweden's GDP during the study period was however approximately 3.5 percent, 50 percent *higher* than agriculture's contribution to GDP in either Germany or the U.K., and only slightly less than in Austria. Thus, while its contribution to European agriculture may be small in absolute terms, the relative contribution of Sweden's agricultural sector to its national GDP is not.

Interest Groups and Policy Choice

The farming lobby is uniquely strong in Sweden. Approximately 85 percent of Sweden's farmers were members of the Federation of Swedish Farmers (LRF) during the study period, and they are formally represented in policy making. Moreover, unlike their counterparts in other countries, Swedish farmers are also members of co-ops that process and market their agricultural products. They own the major slaughterhouses, they dominate the dairy industry, and they are the majority grain processors. According to the LRF, "Farmer owned industry encompasses 16 different sectors, based on some 80 companies with more than 100 wholly or partly owned subsidiaries in Sweden and abroad. The major sectors are purchasing and marketing, meat processing and marketing, dairy farming and forestry. Products are sold under well-known brand names, some of which enjoy an almost institutional status in the Swedish market. These companies have a solid reputation and are market leaders in virtually all of their areas in the Nordic region."[2] Given the breadth of influence of the LRF, and the usual expectations regarding the power of interest groups, it is not surprising that historically Sweden had one of the most protected agricultural sectors in the industrialized world. Swedish agriculture is also among the world's most heavily subsidized, ranking behind only that of Japan, Switzerland, Norway, and Finland.[3]

At the beginning of the period under study, Swedish agricultural policy was similar to that of the European Community (EC). Swedish policy shared the fundamental goals of the EC, i.e., income maintenance and increased production to achieve food security, and employed the same instruments to achieve those goals. Prices were set higher than the world market level; import levies protected domestic farmers; and the extension service advocated methods to increase production, including heavy agrochemical use. The societal results were the same as well. Farmers specialized, land was consolidated, the income gap between farmers of small and large farms increased, high agricultural production generated expensive surpluses, and Swedish consumers paid high food prices.[4]

These policies also generated the same environmental problems experienced elsewhere. Subsidies for capital investment encouraged intensive livestock operations that concentrated many animals in small areas and created excess nitrogen problems from manure. High product prices encouraged the use of chemicals as substitutes for crop rotations and other traditional practices that had historically helped to control pests and preserve the soil. Together with export subsidies, these instruments facilitated specialization and generated monocultures that reduced biodiversity and relied heavily on chemical inputs.[5]

And by the early 1980s, there was growing recognition in Sweden, as elsewhere, that agriculture was causing serious environmental problems. Some of the first debates occurred over the use of nontherapeutic antibiotics and growth hormones in livestock and the overuse of pesticides. To investigate these concerns, the Social Democrats established a "Food Commission" in 1983 to explore the issue of agricultural reform and pesticide use. The 1985 legislation that resulted included environmental and health goals in agriculture policy for the first time.[6]

Policies Affecting Agrochemical Use

Many significant policies affect agrochemical use in Sweden. The government imposed taxes and fees on fertilizers and pesticides in the early 1980s, it funded extension and research focused on minimizing agrochemical use, it subsidized ecological farming methods and shifts to organic production, and it imposed some of the most restrictive chemical registration requirements in the world, including mandatory recertification of all pesticides under the "substitution principle."[7] The substitution principle inhibits, and sometimes precludes, the recertification of a chemical if a more benign alternative is available. The government also required all those that apply pesticides to be trained and certified, and the efficiency of spraying equipment be verified. Perhaps most important, the government mandated a 75-percent reduction in pesticide use from the average 1981–85 level by 1995.

Only the major policies affecting agrochemical use will be covered here. But the breadth of the policy instruments listed above indicates the encompassing nature of measures that were taken, and the use of multiple instruments to protect the environment. Some instruments, namely taxes, fees, registration requirements, and sprayer certification, impose clear costs on farmers and agrochemical manufacturers and are therefore explored in depth. Others, like assistance for nonchemical production and the maintenance of extensive landscapes, are not as directly costly to farmers, but as was seen in the case of Austria, they change farmers' incentives, encourage farmers to produce environmental goods, and facilitate behavioral "fixes" that often affect farmers' perception of the need for environmental protection in the future.

ENVIRONMENTAL TAXES In its 1983 report to the government, the Food Commission proposed the introduction of charges on fertilizers and pesticides. While there was some disagreement among the participants, the committee eventually agreed to base the system on weight of active ingredient sold. In 1984 the government instituted a tax of 4 Swedish Kroner (SEK)/kg of active ingredients that was imposed on all pesticide products except wood preservatives, and a 5-percent tax on nitrogen to induce less use. The revenue from these taxes was used for research on reduced chemical techniques, improved nutrient management, soil testing, and extension advice on fertilization.[8] In 1986 an additional "price regulation fee" of 29 SEK/hectare and applied dose was introduced for agricultural pesticides to reduce the use of pesticides, reduce surpluses, and fund exports.[9]

Other pesticide charges fell directly on agrochemical manufacturers. An application fee of 10,000 SEK was required from companies when they wanted to introduce a new product to the market, and an additional 30,000 SEK was collected if the product contained a new active ingredient. After approval, a registration fee of 1.8 percent of the product's previous year's sales (not less than 2,000 SEK or more than 200,000 SEK) was required annually. These charges were paid to the Chemicals Inspectorate (KemI), the agency responsible for chemical registration, to cover its costs for the approval and the registration of pesticides.[10]

In 1986 and 1987, two government-appointed working groups conducted additional studies on the use of pesticides and fertilizers. One group considered differentiated charges based on product hazard, but decided that differentiated fees would be too difficult to implement. Instead, the committee chose to raise the existing environmental taxes and regulation fees. The environmental tax on pesticides was raised to 8 SEK/kg in 1988, and the regulation fee was raised to 38 SEK in 1990, and then to 46 SEK in 1991. The regulation fee was later reduced to its original level, and then abolished the following year.[11] In 1988, the tax on nitrogen fertilizers was also increased to 10 percent.[12]

According to the LRF, the 30-percent nitrogen tax and levy generated a 10-percent decrease in use, because "it has focused the farmers on using the precise amount."[13] Interestingly, studies indicate that this reduction is more than is economically optimum at that level of tax.[14] The Swedish Board of Agriculture[15] has estimated that the price regulation fee and environmental tax on pesticides generated reductions in use amounting to 80–180 metric tons. The use of fungicides and insecticides was particularly elastic.[16] Again, as with nitrogen fertilizers, farmers have cut usage more than economic analyses would have indicated.[17] This suggests that the psychological importance of the charges on pesticides were underestimated. The charges defined pesticides as serious environmental pollutants, they drove farmers to change their behavior to avoid highly visible costs, and they fostered a desire to create the cleanest and most economical agriculture possible.[18]

THE PESTICIDE REDUCTION PROGRAMS After enacting agrochemical taxes in 1986, the government asked the Swedish Board of Agriculture, KemI,[19] and the Swedish Environmental Protection Agency to develop a program to reduce the health and the environmental risks associated with agricultural pesticide use.[20] The plan developed by these groups became the first of three comprehensive pesticide reduction programs in Sweden. The programs utilized a host of policy instruments that imposed visible costs on farmers and agrochemical suppliers including mandated reductions, stringent registration requirements, education and research, field courses and demonstration farms, and training and equipment certification.

Mandated Reductions in Use The parties decided early on that risk reduction would be measured in kilograms of active ingredients used per hectare. The goal of the first reduction program was a 50-percent reduction from the 1981–85 average by 1990. That initial goal was met by the 1990 deadline. A second reduction program sought an additional 50-percent reduction by 1996, i.e., a total of a 75-percent reduction from the average 1981–85 level.[21] While not quite meeting its ambitious goal, by 1995 Sweden did achieve a 68-percent reduction in use from the 1981–85 average.[22]

Despite the unarguable evidence that the policy instruments chosen were impressively effective, the policy was initially criticized for equating risk with the weight of active ingredient.[23] Clearly not all active ingredients are equally toxic, and it is conceivable that a high dose of one pesticide may be less environmentally harmful than a low dose of another. It is, however, also true that newer products generally require comparatively small doses, i.e., less active ingredient per hectare, and are in general less harmful to the environment. Newer products also tend to be "pest specific," rather than broad spectrum, which is good for biodiversity, and they must also meet stringent standards for biodegradability. Thus, while reducing the amount of active ingredients applied to agricultural land is not necessarily equal to reducing risk, the parties believed it to be a very close proxy. This is especially the case where mandated reductions in quantities of active agreements are paired with the mandated substitution of environmentally dangerous products with less dangerous products, as "a reduction in quantities is also linked to a reduction in risks."[24]

Nevertheless, KemI recognized that measuring the quantity of active ingredients is not the same as measuring risk and therefore attempted to create indicators based on toxicity. In its study, two separate indicators, one for environmental risks and one for risks to human health, were created and then used to evaluate the efficacy of the quantity measures in use. The author found that both of the risk indicators developed did in fact closely mirror the quantity measure, and therefore risk can be equated with the quantity of active ingredient used.[25]

Pesticide Registration The pesticide reduction program also relied on new legal measures, one of the most important being the 1985 Ordinance on Pesticides. That ordinance required that all agricultural chemicals be relicensed every five years.[26] KemI also tightened standards and instituted a rigorous procedure of risk-benefit analysis.[27] The five-year relicensing requirement mandated by the 1985 legislation forced the reregistration of all pesticides used in Sweden between 1990 and 1994. Four hundred and fifty products were reregistered on schedule. In the end, one hundred active ingredients were approved and thirty were rejected due to high health and environmental risks. Importantly, the same documentation was required for both existing and new pesticides, and as a result manufacturers did not apply for renewed approval for 160 older products containing fifty active ingredients.[28] In the end, the relicensing requirement reduced the number of registered products in Sweden from 700 to 350.[29]

The Substitution Principle The 1985 legislation also stipulated that the need for a pesticide should always be evaluated vis-à-vis other nonchemical techniques.[30] The requirement to assess alternatives in order to minimize harm applies to alternative chemicals as well. According to the Swedish Act on Chemical Products (SFS 1985:426), section five: "Anyone handling or importing a chemical product must take such steps and otherwise observe such precautions as are needed to prevent or minimise harm to human beings or to the environment. This includes avoiding chemical products for which less hazardous substitutes are available."[31] KemI interprets, "anyone" to mean everyone, i.e., "manufacturer, user, and authorities when authorisations are considered."[32]

During the reassessment of products between 1990 and 1994, KemI used the substitution principle to refuse approval of some products when alternative products deemed to pose fewer risks were available. Critics argued that the substitution principle imposed unacceptable costs on agrochemical manufacturers, and could even threaten crops by encouraging pesticide resistance due to the limited number of products used. KemI argued that these criticisms were unfounded. The substitution principle is generally applied during the reregistration process; KemI does not revoke the approval of an existing product immediately upon the approval of a new, less-hazardous product that could act as its substitute. This lag not only protects manufacturers, but it also allows the authorities time to ascertain that new products perform well.[33] Moreover, only *significant* differences in risk trigger the substitution principle: "Only when the comparative assessment results in significant differences between the alternatives with respect to risk is approval denied. On the other hand, the mere fact that comparative assessment with respect to risks is made in Sweden, most probably restrains companies from applying for authorisation of pesticides for less favourable alternatives" (Bernson 1997:4).

Thus, in contrast to the implications of critics, many fungible products may be on the market simultaneously, minimizing the likelihood of pest resistance. KemI authorities also argue that the process not only inhibits companies from requesting approval for less-safe products, it actually creates incentives for new product development by providing a guaranteed market for less-hazardous and nonchemical plant protection products.[34] On a more theoretical level, KemI authorities contend that product comparison with respect to risk imposes no greater burden on manufacturers than comparison with respect to efficacy, which is used during the registration process in most countries.[35]

Moreover, if a product is removed from the market due to invocation of the substitution principle, there may be compensation. The Swedish Association of Agrochemical Manufacturers feels that while substitution may hurt an individual manufacturer, it does not threaten the industry as a whole. The association also agrees with KemI that the substitution principle is likely to encourage the development of new, more environmentally friendly products.[36] It should also be noted that new products are usually more profitable for the manufacturers than those withdrawn.[37]

Dosage Testing and Labeling Part of the registration process after 1985 required that KemI evaluate products not just at the manufacturers' recommended dose rates, as was customary, but at lower dose rates as well:

> dose testing of at least two doses lower than those requested by the manufacturer and where possible the lower doses were

to be added to the product label with their associated levels of efficacy. . . . Where weed species did not respond uniformly, dose responses for individual species were added to product labels.. .. There was a general perception that over-application of pesticides was commonplace because manufacturers recommended best performance doses and growers often increased rates additionally.[38]

The fact that recommended dose rates were designed to produce the best results under the worst conditions was only one reason that rates could often be lowered substantially. The other reason was that the manufacturers' standard for efficacy, or "best results," and therein its basis for dose rate recommendations, is determined by the number of surviving weeds after application, rather than on the weed densities after application. Weed density, however, is the crucial determinant for yields.[39] Therefore, "herbicide efficacy" is actually a poor indicator of crop yield. Thus, labeling regulations that required manufacturers to list efficacy rates of lower dosages became an important part of the registration procedure.[40]

Research and Extension Determining the most efficacious dose rates for new and existing products required extensive field trials and research. That work is done at the Swedish University of Agricultural Sciences in Uppsala, which trains researchers, teachers, and high-level agricultural advisors. The university was an essential partner in the pesticide reduction programs. Using revenues from agrochemical taxes, research funding increased substantially, and, in 1987–88, 12 percent of state support for agricultural research was environmentally oriented.[41] The new focus emphasized nonchemical methods of plant protection, including rotations, and improved use of herbicides.[42] Also included was a research program on the persistence and leaching of chemicals, instituted to inform KemI's decisions on registration.[43] KemI also sponsored research on low-risk substitutes to replace old pesticides, which ultimately eliminated many of the most hazardous products.[44]

When the University of Agricultural Sciences went through its field trial files, it found substantial documentation revealing that the best yields were achieved at half the manufacturers' recommended dose. Half dose rates eliminated between 70 and 80 percent of the weeds in a field.[45] While higher doses of herbicides may eliminate more weeds, they can also damage crops and, as a result, lower yields. Research also demonstrated that crop rotations and other nonchemical farming practices can be used to lower dose rates.[46]

The dissemination of this information to farmers was critical to the success of the programs.[47] Revenues from agrochemical taxes, and support from KemI, allowed the expansion of the extension service. Five regional plant protection centers were established to run field trials and train extension officers in lower dose rates and nonchemical methods, so they could, in turn, educate farmers.[48] Voluntary educational field trials with full, half, and quarter dose applications were conducted across the country. A major effort was made by the extension service to impress upon growers the concept of "less is best." Field trials allowed agricultural researchers and extension officers to demonstrate that farmers could *reduce* their use of some herbicides by one half and see a slight *increase* in yields. In 1988–89, 350 field trials were conducted to demonstrate that while manufacturers' recommended dosage rates provided superior weed control, they also damaged crops and depressed yields.[49] The Swedish Board of Agriculture also initiated programs and supported the advisory service. Field courses and demonstration trials, about 200 per year since 1989, stressed the possibilities of reducing dose rates, and served as an important source of information for farmers.[50] In 1993–94 there were also 300 field or farm courses with approximately 7,000 participants, 100 other courses attracting 3,500 participants, and about 550 analyses of individual farms.[51] As a product of these demonstration trials and field courses, significantly lower doses of pesticides were used by farmers, especially in the case of herbicides.[52]

Organic Production The Swedish government also devoted research and extension funds to organic production, and the state provided two days of free advice on organic farming.[53] Beginning in 1989, the government paid farmers who switched to organic farming the same as if they had "set-aside" land. Direct payments were also made to allow a five-year phaseout of chemical use, after which land had to be managed without chemicals for an additional six years. The program quadrupled the amount of land under organic production in its first year.[54]

Training and Equipment Certification A final element of the pesticide reduction programs was testing the equipment used to apply pesticides and certifying all those who use such equipment. "Agricultural scientists estimated that a 25 percent reduction in pesticide use could be achieved through sprayer precision. . . . Sprayer calibration tests conducted between 1982 and 1984 indicated that in 422 tested sprayers, 52 percent had faulty nozzles and 26 percent more had pump or delivery problems."[55] A voluntary program for testing of old and new sprayers went into effect in 1988. The government and the LRF subsidized both the construction of mobile sprayer testing units and the tests themselves.[56] Grants were given to farmers and companies for the costs of carrying out the tests, and for purchasing or rebuilding test equipment. Fixed subsidies of SEK 1,000 per farmer initially covered about 75 percent of the cost for farmers, and companies were reimbursed 50 percent (up to 50,000 SEK) for the actual cost of purchasing or rebuilding test equipment.[57] Between 1988 and 1992 about 160 examiners were trained to conduct tests, and about 6,000, or an estimated 40 percent of the sprayers used in Sweden were tested.[58] Beginning in 1991 new strict guidelines for precision and performance were established for all new spray equipment, and testing of new sprayers has been mandatory.[59] By 1998 a total of approximately 18,000 tests had been performed, and about 305 examiners had been trained.[60]

Farmers must also be trained to use equipment properly. Beginning in 1988, six different courses were offered depending on the type of production.[61] Beginning in 1990 all farmers who spray pesticides professionally were required to be certificated to operate equipment. A mandatory three-day course, which costs farmers the U.S. equivalent of about $35–$40 per day, educates farmers on the risks pesticides pose to human health and the environment, and provides them with information on the use of nonchemical methods of pest control. Farmers must pass a test at the conclusion of the course, and recertification, which requires a one-day refresher course, is required every five years. Between 1988 and 1990, 20,000 people completed the course;[62] by 1997, that figure increased to 30,000.[63] Not only was the course intended to ensure proficiency in chemical and equipment use, it was also designed to make farmers more cognizant of the health and environmental risks of pesticides, because "better knowledge by the farmers can substitute for use of pesticides."[64]

Results In the end, it was estimated that approximately 25 percent of Sweden's reduction in agrochemical use was due to the substitution of old hazardous pesticides with new, less-hazardous products. Another 25 percent of the reduction was due to lower application rates and better working equipment, and 50 percent of the reduction was due to the substitution of phenoxy-acids herbicides with other herbicides which are used at a much lower rate.[65] Importantly, the significant reduction in agrochemical use did not hinder production; cereal yields did not decrease and the net costs to farmers were small. In fact, reduced agrochemical use was often profitable, especially with reduced rates of herbicides.[66] According to the Organization for Economic Cooperation and Development (OECD), "The fall in the use of fertilisers and pesticides was very significant up to 1992 . . . . there does not seem to have been a commensurate or indeed any fall in yields as have been expected in response to such large declines in application rates."[67]

Interestingly, few attribute the success of the programs to the introduction of taxes on agrochemicals. There is near universal agreement that dramatic reduction in use was due to the shift toward newer low dose products and the reduction in the rates at which farmers applied agrochemicals. Clearly, however, environmental taxes not only provided the funds for research and extension, which is important in itself, they also sent a message to farmers that agrochemicals were potentially serious pollutants— a message that many farmers in other countries have yet to receive. This is not to say that taxes and fees were entirely responsible for the success of the programs. Stringent registration legislation, the mandatory reregistration of all existing products, the adoption of the substitution principle, state-sponsored research, and farmer education, training, and certification requirements were all essential ingredients. However, the dramatic success of the Swedish program, especially in light of crop yields, begs the question: Why were these policies chosen in Sweden and not elsewhere?

The Determinants of Agrochemical Use

The answers from the field do not locate the root of the explanation in *who* makes agrochemical choice, as farmers did in the British case, or *where* decisions were made, as we found in both Germany and Austria, but in *how* policy is made. Over and over again, when asked about the fundamental element that drove the successful greening of agricultural policy, interviewees representing all groups cited the broad cooperation of competing groups in the formation and implementation of policy.

Unlike the other countries studied, Swedish environmental and agricultural interests have focused on their common goals during implementation of policy. The Swedish EPA enjoys a "good relationship" with the Federation of Swedish Farmers and the Board of Agriculture.[68] An Agriculture Ministry official stated that neither the opposition political parties nor farmers were opposed to pesticide regulations because "safety and health are important to farmers," and all groups work together to that end (Svedinger 1999). Even the director of the Association of Swedish Plant and Wood Protection Industries, the representative of Swedish agrochemical manufacturers, felt that groups worked together more in Sweden than they did in other countries "because we see that we have the same goal and we focus on that" (Ljunggren 1999). Perhaps the Officer of Agriculture for the Swedish Society for Nature Conservation said it best when she was discussing her group's relationship with the LRF: "When I compare that with other European colleagues they say 'wow'—for them this is unthinkable" (Rudquist 1999).

Academics have come to the same conclusion when looking for an explanation for the success of Swedish agrochemical policy. "Superior cooperation between farmers, agricultural scientists, environmentalists and policy makers, combined with financial support for research and extension services allowed Sweden to meet its goals in an environmentally and economically sustainable way."[69] Cooperation is the key. The question is, why do groups cooperate in Sweden when those same groups do not cooperate in other countries?

Government-Directed Consensus

Groups with conflicting interests do not work together of their own accord. Since the 1940s, Swedish governments have relied on a policy formation process that demands cooperation between groups that would otherwise compete for policy influence. When the government wants to investigate a problem and potentially make new policy it issues a directive and names a special commission to analyze the situation, evaluate current policy, and recommend modifications. The commission's report is circulated for comment from all interested actors, the government submits its proposal based on that input, the proposal is reviewed and modified in parliamentary committee, and then Parliament votes on proposed policy changes in plenary session.[70] The integration of environmental concerns in agricultural policy reform has been no exception. In this instance, the government commissioned the Board of Agriculture to study the issue and required that the board cooperate with the Chemicals Inspectorate and the Swedish EPA. This type of direction is the normal initiation process when a Swedish government wants to make new policy. The groups responsible may also choose to include other groups in the process. It is the cooperation between groups at this initial stage of the process that creates a consensus on policy goals and the instruments that will achieve desired ends.

Because governments of all partisan stripes rely heavily on this same process of delegation and intergroup compromise, policy making is less politicized and less partisan than in countries where one party is responsible for policy choice and the policy influence of specific interest groups varies with the political party(ies) in power. Interest groups in Sweden recognize that they will have to work with each other regardless of which party wins the most votes, and the success or failure of the policy choices they help make will ultimately fall on them.

Conclusion

One of the defining characteristics of Sweden, and the one most closely linked to its policy performance, is its inclusive and consensual policy making. The Swedish corporatist interest group system demands the inclusion of peak organizations that represent all members of a particular sector in policy making, and Sweden's multi-party political system engenders consensual politics and compromise among parties. Yet while both Germany and Austria are characterized by the same institutions, the policy outcomes that resulted in Sweden were substantially different than in those two cases.

Swedish governments were able to induce far greater reductions in the use of agrochemicals than any country studied. Moreover, this outcome was clearly achieved through legislation that imposed multiple concentrated costs on farmers and agrochemical manufacturers, costs that were not compensated for with the creation of other programs. The economists' dismissal of the direct economic efficiency of agrochemical charges notwithstanding, the costs of pesticide registration were financed by increased manufacturers' fees, and agrochemical taxes paid for university research and extension services that conducted field trials on the efficacy of lower dosage rates.[71] The knowledge farmers acquired as a result of these programs allowed them to use agrochemicals more safely and more efficaciously as well, with both environmental and economic benefits.[72] In addition, the education, training and certification requirements imposed on farmers left them far better educated and with more efficient equipment than their counterparts in any other country studied.

The most obvious explanation for those differences is the concentration of authority that derives from the unitary organization of the Swedish state. It is perhaps nowhere as clear as in an investigation of the agricultural sector that a unitary state structure limits the ability of regional interests to avoid concentrated costs. Policy preferences emanating from the different agricultural situations in the north and south of Sweden did not dilute national policy goals or shift the costs of policy change during implementation as they did in Germany. Regional interests associated with forestry, dairy production, and arable crops were not able to protect their particular interests or weaken national policy as similarly situated interests did in Austria. As this and other theories of interest group influence anticipate, the centralization of authority in Sweden appears to have limited the influence of regionally focused interest groups that were able to influence outcomes in the federal states studied.

Yet, like the Austrian case study before it, the Swedish case study also confirms that policy change occurred only when institutions obscured responsibility for policy choice so parties could impose costs on their own constituencies. The positive relationship between policy change and obscured responsibility is more important than federalism theoretically, and given the British example of concentrated authority in a single-party majority government, multi-party decision making explains greater policy variance empirically.

Minority Representation and the Majority Interest

In direct contrast to veto-based theories of interest group influence, the Swedish case demonstrates that it was *not* the exclusion of specific groups that was associated with the imposition of costs, but the *inclusion* of multiple minority interests that allowed policy change. While the Social Democrats were in government alone during most of the period, the policy reform of the late 1980s is explicitly described as a product of "coalition" negotiations to which the Social Democrats agreed because they needed support on their economic package.[73] In describing the politics behind the latest agricultural reform, Vail et al. state: "The Social Democrats had an interest in pushing through a pro-consumer reform without bearing sole responsibility for any negative consequences. It was also in the bourgeois parties' interests to reach a consensus that would avoid later inter-coalition conflicts, in case they should win the 1991 general election and form a government" (1994:185). They also argue that multi-party policy making had a decisive impact on interest group strategies. The farmers' union refused to discuss any alternative to the existing policy of high price supports prior to the 1990 reform, "but when the multi-party support for deregulation became clear, LRF shifted its focus" (Vail et al. 1994:185).

Given the dominance of the Social Democratic Party during the study period, this case also demonstrates that the ideological preferences of parties in government, or supporting governments, were unrelated to ultimate policy choice. The Social Democrats were the lone party in a minority government when they created the "Food Commission" in 1983 and remained in power throughout the subsequent pesticide reduction programs and accompanying legislation. Although a party of the left, and therein often assumed to have pro-environment positions, the Social Democrats—referred to as "the party of concrete"—had a voting record that was among the least "environmental" at the time, and the party was not seen as being "green."[74, 75] And, ironically, it was the "small government" Liberal Party that advocated agrochemical taxes and paying farmers for environmental goods.

In conclusion, as unintuitive as it may have been at the outset, it is clear from the case study, alone and in comparison to those that came before, that the design of Swedish political institutions significantly affected farmers' use of pesticides and fertilizers in their fields. The combination of a unitary state and proportional electoral system generated a multi-party system in which single-party minority or coalition governments could impose costs—even on their own constituents—because institutionalized compromise and cooperation at the national level provided political cover. Interest groups were unable to wield decisive power over political parties in this environment. It is no surprise, then, that when I asked why Swedish agrochemical policy was so different from that found in most other countries, the representatives of the LRF responded, "The difference is the government" (Eksvard, Sandrup, and Persson 1999).

9

INSTITUTIONAL DESIGN AND THE QUALITY
OF DEMOCRACY

> Government must not only respond to interest group demands; it
> must be able to resist them and mediate among them as well. . . .
> Representativeness requires that parties speak to and for these conflicting
> interests; governability requires that parties have sufficient autonomy to
> rise above them.
> —Larry Diamond, *Three Paradoxes of Democracy* 1990

Diamond argued that one of the great paradoxes of democracy is
that the political institutions that facilitate representation simultaneously
inhibit governability. The "universal tension" between representativeness
and governability he described has become an axiom of institutional theory
and a fundamental assumption when anticipating the trade-offs inherent
in institutional design.

The political institution that has the greatest impact on both representativeness and governability is the electoral system, because it determines
both the threshold for representation and the number of political parties
that must normally cooperate to make policy. While we recognize that
small parties may be necessary to faithfully represent diverse interests in
society, we also expect that the inclusion of minorities in policy making
may compromise government's ability to impose costs on small groups
when necessary to respond to the needs of the majority.

This expectation is based on two separate assumptions. The first is that
small parties will attempt to veto policy change that imposes costs on their

narrow constituencies. The second assumption is that large parties that represent electoral majorities, especially those that are empowered to govern alone, will enact policies that benefit majorities because their majority status provides the autonomy necessary to resist the demands of small groups.

Yet decades of empirical research on advanced democracies finds little evidence to support these assumptions. Political institutions that concentrate policy-making authority in large parties do not outperform political systems that offer greater representation. It does not matter if political power is concentrated in a single majority party at the national level alone, or divided among majority parties in multiple political bodies; large parties are not demonstrably less vulnerable to the demands of small organized groups, nor are they superior providers of majority-preferred policies. Moreover, political systems normally governed by coalitions of relatively small parties are not hampered in their ability to provide for the majority; in fact, the evidence suggests the reverse. Contrary to theoretical expectations, government capacity to "rise above" interest groups when necessary to enact needed policy change appears be greater in political systems that empower small parties than it is in political systems that concentrate power in a single party.

The vulnerability thesis introduced in this book offers an explanation for unexpected patterns of policy choice in democratic polities, one that questions our core assumptions about the relative political vulnerability of representatives who lead small and large parties. It requires us to put aside conventional expectations about how institutions facilitate majority and minority representation, and ask instead how institutions affect the ability of small groups to punish politicians for unpopular choices. The approach reveals a surprisingly simple answer: Politicians are vulnerable to interest group influence where attentive groups can identify those responsible for policy choice and hold politicians accountable at the polls.

Ironically, the model anticipates that vulnerability will be greatest in political systems that concentrate power in the majority because the institutions that facilitate majority rule also make policy makers identifiable and accountable for their choices. Politicians are, by contrast, relatively invulnerable to pressure groups where institutions facilitate minority representation because these institutions obscure responsibility for policy choice and limit electoral accountability, inhibiting political retribution by organized groups.

Linking identifiability and accountability to interest group influence generates expectations diametrically opposed to those of existing theories. The continuum of political vulnerability developed in chapter two anticipates the greatest interest group influence in parliamentary systems that use single-member district (SMD) elections. Existing theories predict that interest groups will be weakest under these institutions. The theory also anticipates that interest groups would have the least influence in multi-party systems that empower small parties because these political systems inhibit electoral accountability and obscure identifiability for policy choice. As a result, the thesis suggests that it is through the representation of minorities that governments find the political cover necessary to rise above the demands of organized groups. It also suggests that the fragility of majorities under majority rule is governability's Achilles' heel.

Testing the Theory

Designing research to test an institutional theory of interest group influence is challenging, especially when the institution argued to be the source of interest group influence is the electoral system. The problem is that cross-national differences in the electoral system tend to co-vary with both the modal government ideology and the system of interest group representation. Political systems that use proportional representation (PR) tend to produce governments of the left, and they are also strongly associated with corporatist interest group systems. Political systems that use SMD elections tend to produce governments of the right, and they are associated with pluralist interest group systems. This is important because cross-national differences in interest group preferences or government ideology could arguably account for cross-national differences in many of the policy choices commonly studied.

Given these two considerations, cross-national differences in agrochemical policies presented an excellent opportunity to conduct the first critical test of the theory. Not only is agriculture one of the few policy arenas where differences between pluralist and corporatist interest group systems are unimportant theoretically, protecting the environment from agrochemical contamination has been accepted as a government responsibility for decades.

Cross-national differences in policy choice and changes in the use of agrochemicals reported in chapter three strongly supported the model. International reviews of policy choice revealed dramatic differences among comparable countries. While a majority of the political systems that used PR enacted stringent policies to reduce agrochemical use, no significant policies were reported for political systems that rely exclusively on SMD elections. The statistical analyses of trends in agrochemical use were equally definitive. The quantitative analysis indicated that formal political institutions have a significant impact on trends in agrochemical use, statistically and substantively, controlling for changes in cropping patterns, the economic power of affected industry groups, and public opinion.

Although linkages between formal political institutions and farmers' use of fertilizers and pesticides are not intuitive, the correlation between policy choice and measurable reductions in agrochemical use was not surprising. The vulnerability thesis predicts that institutions will affect politicians' incentives to enact policies that impose concentrated costs on powerful groups, and those policies predictably affect farmers' incentives to use agrochemicals in the field. Nevertheless, quantitative analysis of agrochemical data can only tell us so much. In-depth case studies were necessary to deepen our understanding of the policymaking process and anticipate alternative explanations for policy choice. Case studies of four European countries were presented for comparative analysis to further investigate how variation in formal political institutions affected interest group influence on policy choice.

Minority Influence and Majority Rule: The United Kingdom

The British political system has long been the model of pure majority-rule. Texts on political institutions often begin with the British case because the relationship between the government and the governed is nowhere as simple or transparent. In Britain, the representative that wins the most votes in each district wins the right to represent the district, and the party that wins the most seats in parliament wins the right to elect the executive. The single-party majority government that is normally formed does not have to compromise with other political parties or lower levels of government to make policy. Identifiability is therefore very high, as is accountability—everyone knows who is responsible for policy choice and voters can easily remove individual representatives from power, and the parties they serve, at the polls. For that reason theorists generally argue that the first-past-the-post parliamentary system is most likely to foster incentives for politicians to transmit the preferences of a majority of voters into policy choice.

Bringing interest groups into the analysis questioned the simple linkage between identifiable and accountable governments and majority preferred outcomes. Contrary to conventional wisdom, the vulnerability thesis anticipates that SMDs will advantage small groups because SMD competition allows interest groups to identify and punish politicians for unfavorable policy choices.

The history of agrochemical policymaking in the U.K. proved unfailingly—and almost uncomfortably—consistent with this expectation. Despite world-wide concern with the environmental consequences of agrochemical use and strong public support for environmental protection domestically, British governments were unwilling to impose any costs on farmers or agrochemical manufacturers during the study period. The only British policies enacted to reduce agrochemical use were driven by European Union directives and relied entirely on voluntary compliance. The convoluted determination of Nitrate Vulnerable Zones described in chapter five was particularly telling. British governments not only expended substantial public resources to avoid enacting policies that imposed costs on farmers, Britain was ultimately brought before the European Court of Justice for its failure to implement the directive. Given these facts, it is no surprise that agrochemical use increased in Britain throughout the period.

The case study also revealed two unexpected determinants of agrochemical use. The first is British farmers' heavy (and unique) reliance on the chemical distributors for agricultural advice. Unlike any other country studies, the vast majority of British farmers relied exclusively on "crop-walkers," who sold fertilizers and pesticides for pest management advice. Exacerbating industry influence, the British government reduced government provision of agricultural advice during the 1980s, despite wide recognition that the agricultural sector needed more diverse information, especially on conservation (Winter 1997:371–72). The second unexpected determinant of agrochemical use were private supermarket protocols that required farmers to limit their use of agrochemicals. The creation of supermarket protocols is notable in a majoritarian system because they demonstrate that the absence of government regulation was contrary to public's preferences.

Majority Influence Where Minorities Rule: Sweden and Austria

Policymaking in Sweden provided a striking contrast to that in Britain. Swedish politicians imposed a multiplicity of significant concentrated costs on both farmers and chemical manufactures in order to achieve ambitious reduction targets in the use of pesticides and fertilizers. Moreover, Sweden's unparalleled accomplishment in reducing agrochemical use to little more than a quarter of what it was before the imposition of costs was widely attributed to government action. Governments set reduction targets of 50 and then 75 percent, and they enacted stringent agrochemical registration requirements that cut the number of products on the market by half. In addition, they enacted multiple agrochemical taxes that generated immediate changes in the use of inputs. Finally, Swedish governments funded extensive education and research programs to facilitate long-term changes in farmer behavior.

When asked how Sweden was able to achieve these remarkable results, members from all groups pointed to the way policy was made, specifically the fact that Swedish governments require that all affected groups participate in the formation of new policies. Importantly, however, despite the formal inclusion of comparatively powerful agricultural interests in every phase of policy making, decision makers were able to impose significant costs on farmers, one of the most power actors in domestic politics, and one of the most powerful farmers' unions in the world.

While veto-based models also anticipate greater public good provision in unitary and parliamentary systems that use PR elections, these theories explicitly assume that greater spending on public goods is due to greater representation of minority interests. In contrast, the vulnerability thesis anticipates greater public goods provision in these systems precisely because PR makes parties invulnerable to retribution, including punishment by powerful groups within their own constituencies. It is therefore important to note that Swedish governments enacted policies against the stated preferences of the largest and most powerful political party, the

Social Democrats. This fact supports the argument that the key to cost imposition, especially on a party's own constituents, is multi-party decision making that normally results from PR.

The Austrian case study provided additional evidence in this regard. Recall that Austria was chosen for analysis in large part because it has a unique history of PR producing both single-party majority governments and coalition governments. The timing of policy change was therefore noteworthy. Neither taxes nor subsidies were used during the period of single-party majority governments of the left that governed during the height of environmentalism from 1970 to 1983. And while agrochemical taxes were first imposed by a coalition government during a period when it was losing votes to the Green Party, it was not until the two large parties governed together in a grand coalition in 1986 that they were able to act in opposition to the interests of powerful social partners and enact policies that ultimately altered farmers' behavior.

How Federalism Matters: Policy Choice in Austria and Germany

Like veto-based theories, the vulnerability thesis anticipates that federalism will inhibit cost imposition on geographically concentrated groups. Unlike conventional theories however, the vulnerability-based model depicts federalism as the least important institutional determinant of policy choice. Policymaking processes in Austria and Germany supported the expectation that the electoral system will be the most important determinant of government vulnerability to small groups, but it also suggested that federalism may play a more complex role than the thesis anticipated. Federalism allowed farmers in both countries to shift the burden of costs imposed at the national level to the public at large. While environmental goals were ultimately achieved in each case, sub-national actors were able to mitigate the costs in similar ways.

In Germany, local authorities shifted the costs of environmental protection from farmers, the source of the problem, to water suppliers. Farmers were compensated for using fewer agrochemicals through cooperative agreements with water suppliers, who were charged to reduce water pollution by the state. Farmers were also paid not to pollute in Austria. For farmers in the mountainous regions, the government provided direct financial "compensation" for ecological farming methods through agricultural policy. For farmers in flat regions, the government rebated fertilizer taxes via export subsidies and tax relief on diesel fuels.

Given that formal political institutions rarely change, policy making in Austria and Germany offers valuable lessons for those who seek to protect the environment. Both case studies suggest that, where governments are vulnerable, the most efficient way to achieve some environmental goals may be to pay the polluter to stop polluting. Readers may recall that the only instruments that proved effective in reducing agrochemical pollution in Britain were the voluntary Nitrate Sensitive Areas schemes that also paid farmers not to pollute. Compensating powerful groups for policy change may not be principled or perceived as fair, but paying the polluter is a politically easy option and may therefore be the best route to change where institutions inhibit governments from imposing concentrated costs.

Future Research

The vulnerability thesis is a general model of interest group influence on policy choice. While great care was taken to identify a policy area that allowed a decisive test of the theory, the thesis offers a potential explanation for policy variance across a wide variety of policy domains. While cross-national differences in ideology and the system of interest group representation can influence policy choice, the systematic differences often attributed to these variables may just as easily reflect politicians' vulnerability to interest group pressure instead. Arguably, many policy outcomes are observationally equivalent. Therefore, the thesis begs for testing in other policy areas.

Environmental Policy

The most obvious place to conduct future tests of the model is on environmental performance measures wherever environmental protection requires the imposition of concentrated costs. As discussed in chapter three, there are no private providers of environmental protection, and environmental groups do not enjoy formal access to policy makers in corporatist systems. These two facts reduce the likelihood that modal government ideology and the type of interest group system will obscure the causal relationship between electoral vulnerability and policy choice.

As indicated in the introduction, PR systems are generally associated with better environmental performance across the board, with lower average rates of pollution and lower levels of municipal waste. The vulnerability-based model is well positioned to help us understand the root of these differences because it forces us to ask questions about the political influence of powerful groups before they are known as polluters. Unlike veto-based theories developed to help us examine political change, the vulnerability thesis helps us examine the routine policy choices that allowed small groups to pollute the commons in the first place.

Cross-national differences in the influence of environmental groups also warrant attention. The thesis predicts that interest groups will be more powerful where politicians are politically vulnerable—regardless of the goal of the group. Therefore we should expect that the power of environmental groups will vary with institutional design just as the power of agricultural and business groups did here. It is therefore interesting to note that the relatively greater power of environmental groups in the United States is associated with poorer environmental performance.[1] Some argue that powerful environmental groups limit politicians' ability to respond flexibly to technological change, often demanding command and control regulations where flexibility may be more effective. The inefficacy of inflexible regulations over the long term may help explain why the United States is home to many of the strongest environmental groups in the world yet consistently ranks among the poorest performers on many environmental measures compared to other industrialized democracies.

Recall that the rigidity of environmental goals was also blamed for poor performance in the European Union. The environmental directives reviewed in chapter four were intractable because politicians, especially those elected to the European Parliament, could not be seen as shrinking from the demands of environmental groups that sought irrational water quality standards. The rigidity of the standards was ultimately counterproductive, threatening the credibility of the Environment Directorate and international environmental policy making.

International relations scholars who study multi-national environmental agreements are also likely to find the model useful. It is widely accepted that the preferences of domestic groups can exert strong if not decisive influence their national governments' bargaining positions on environmental treaties.[2] Dai's formal theoretical model is perhaps the most explicit in this regard, and it posits cross-national differences in the power of domestic groups that are consistent with the vulnerability thesis. Dai argues that domestic groups will have greater influence over policy choice where institutions facilitate electoral accountability.[3] The model cannot be fully tested, however, without a method for ranking political systems based on how domestic institutions affect accountability. The vulnerability index offers international relations scholars the perfect instrument to test Dai's conditional model.

Social Policy

The social policies that have historically distinguished policy making in multi-party systems from policy making in two-party systems are especially ripe for re-analysis. One of the most commonly studied social policy arenas where interest group influence has been deemed critical to understanding policy choice is health care policy. It is therefore important to note that the vulnerability-based model is consistent with cross-national differences in the adoption of health care policies generally cited to support veto-based theories. In Immergut's path-breaking work that introduced the veto point paradigm for example, Sweden is depicted as a political system without veto points when the party or parties in government command a legislative majority. She suggests that health care reform was preferred by Social Democrats who were able to enact their policy preferences because the parliamentary system allowed the executive to govern authoritatively. Yet, according to Immergut, when the Social Democrats governed alone with a legislative majority they were unwilling to promote policy change out of fear that future electoral losses could threaten their power. In fact, Immergut emphasized that the Social Democrats waited to pass legislation until when they were not vulnerable electorally.[4]

The vulnerability thesis also offers an alternative explanation for the absence of universal healthcare in the United States. Steinmo and Watts argue that popular majorities have long supported government involvement that would make healthcare available to all citizens. Yet multiple attempts by U.S. presidents to introduce such policies were ultimately thwarted in the legislature, even under unified government when the majority of both houses was held by the president's party.[5] While these repeated failures are consistent with a strict veto-based model of policy choice that anticipates that legislatures can thwart presidential executive's proposals for reform, veto theories do not explain *why* the health care lobby is able to influence legislators to act against the preferences of their constituents and their party. The role of the electoral system on interest group influence begs for further analysis.

Economic Policy

Like cross-national differences in social policy, systematic differences in economic policy are often attributed to government ideology. We cannot ignore the fact that variance in the electoral system is correlated with variance in the ideological complexion of government and the system of interest group representation. Nevertheless, we should remain cognizant of the likelihood that vulnerability-induced differences in interest group influence would affect policy choice in ways indistinguishable from those attributed to distinct political ideologies. The vulnerability thesis provides researchers with an institutional model to reevaluate relationships between policy outcomes and government ideology; relationships that may be obscuring a more fundamental relationship between institutional design and interest group influence.

Where business groups are powerful, for example, we should expect less regulation and fewer government-provided social services if private actors can provide those services at a profit. We should also find higher levels of unemployment, lower inflation, and greater wealth accumulation. Where institutions insulate politicians from retribution by powerful business groups, by contrast, policy makers are more likely to restrict economic activities when necessary to protect the public interest, provide public social services when the public sector can provide services at a lower cost than private providers, and enact higher levels of taxation that redistribute wealth. It is therefore noteworthy that political systems that empower two large parties are associated with low taxes, low consumer prices and low government spending.[6]

Implications for Democratic Theory

Scholars who study government performance find that the quality of democracy varies substantially with institutional design. It is incumbent upon us to ask why. This question brings us to the primary goal of this book, to bring interest groups back into democratic theory. Scholars have anticipated a relationship between interest group influence and the structure of political institutions since Madison argued that institutional engineering could control the effects of faction. Yet despite our best efforts to observe that relationship, conventional models fail to demonstrate the posited effects. The vulnerability thesis offers an explanation for the absence of findings. We are looking in the wrong places. Institutional theories developed to explain representation have focused our attention on the causal mechanisms that explain politicians' relationships with voters or other politicians, not on the mechanisms that explain their relationships with interest groups. As a result, we have conducted a drunkard's search for evidence under the wrong theoretical light.

The vulnerability thesis shifts our focus from how institutions affect politicians' ability to represent groups to how they affect politicians' ability to win reelection. In doing so it casts light on the negative effects of identifiability and accountability. The implications of the theory force us to question the conventional wisdom linking majoritarian decision making with majority-preferred policies, and consider the very real possibility that majorities may be better served by governments comprised of minorities.

As indicated in the introduction to this book, the literature already links PR elections and multiparty government to superior minority representation, greater government congruence with the median voter, higher levels of political sophistication, and better provisions of public goods. Political vulnerability to interest group influence is therefore only one more argument against SMD elections. Yet it is an important one. Majoritarian systems are not designed to represent minorities or produce certain types of outcomes; they are designed to empower politicians to represent the majority's will efficiently. If they fail in that regard, we must question their legitimacy.

NOTES

1. Interest Group Influence and Institutional Design

1. Olson, *Logic of Collective Action.*

2. Olson, *Rise and Decline of Nations.*

3. Ibid., 50–51, qualifies that expectation, however, with the recognition that even where parties are large, policy preferences will reflect the size of the party only if party discipline is strong.

4. Committee on Political Parties, American Political Science Association, "Toward a More Responsible Two-Party System"; Lijphart, *Democracies* and *Patterns of Democracy;* Weaver and Rockman, "Assessing the Effects of Institutions"; Tsebelis, "Decision Making in Political Systems" and *Veto Players;* Cox and McCubbins, "Institutional Determinants of Economic Policy Outcomes"; Mesquita et al., *Logic of Political Survival.*

5. Roller, *Performance of Democracies,* argues that these four broad areas constitute the universe of policy areas for which modern governments are responsible.

6. See Lijphart, *Patterns of Democracy,* for measures of economic and social policy; Brichfield and Crepaz, "Impact of Constitutional Structures and Collective and Competitive Veto Points on Income Inequality in Industrialized Democracies," on inequality; Gerring, Thacker, and Moreno, "Centripetal Theory of Democratic Governance," on public health and social policy; Scruggs, *Sustaining Abundance,* on environmental protection; and Roller, *Performance of Democracies,* for a full spectrum of performance measures of social, economic, and environmental policies. See Persson and Tabellini, *Economic Effects of Constitutions,* for formal models that focus primarily on the relationship between electoral rules and government spending for programs that benefit large segments of the public.

7. Lijphart, *Democracies* and *Patterns of Democracy;* Powell, *Elections as Instruments of Democracy.*

8. Olson, *Rise and Decline of Nations;* Arnold, *Logic of Congressional Action.*

9. Berelson, "Democratic Theory and Public Opinion"; Dimock, *Political Knowledge and Partisanship*. See Granberg and Holmberg, "Berelson Paradox Reconsidered," for the argument that the paradox does not apply in systems with proportional representation.

10. Arnold, *Logic of Congressional Action;* Pierson and Weaver, "Imposing Losses in Pension Policy"; Steinmo and Tolbert, "Do Institutions Really Matter?"; Gerring, Thacker, and Moreno, "Centripetal Theory of Democratic Governance."

11. See Committee on Political Parties; Cox, *Efficient Secret;* Weaver and Rockman, *Do Institutions Matter?;* and Moe and Caldwell, "Institutional Foundations of Democratic Government," for the advantages of parliamentary over presidential regimes. See Olson, *Rise and Decline of Nations;* Birchfield and Crepaz, "Impact of Constitutional Structures"; and Gerring, Thacker, and Moreno, "Centripetal Theory of Democratic Governance," for the advantages of centralized policy-making authority.

12. Huber, Ragin, and Stephens' model of constitutional veto points suggests that individual legislators can act as veto points as well.

13. Weaver and Rockman, "Assessing the Effects of Institutions," 27–28; Cox and McCubbins, "Institutional Determinants of Policy Outcomes," 47.

14. Feigenbaum, Samuels, and Weaver, "Innovation, Coordination, and Implementation in Energy Policy," 107; Gunther and Mughan, "Political Institutions and Cleavage Management," 288; Lijphart, Rogowski, and Weaver, "Separation of Powers and Cleavage Management," 333. Weaver and Rockman, "Institutional Reform and Constitutional Design," 460.

15. Olson, *Rise and Decline of Nations;* Lijphart, *Democracies* and *Patterns of Democracy;* Steinmo, "Political Institutions and Tax Policy," 512; Cox and McCubbins, "Institutional Determinants of Economic Policy Outcomes."

16. For the relationship between federalism and private investment see Lancaster and Hicks, "Impact of Federalism and Neo-corporatism"; for government spending see Keman, "Federalism and Policy Performance"; for the size of the public sector see Cameron, "Expansion of the Public Economy"; Castles and McKinlay, "Does Politics Matter?"; and Schmidt, "When Parties Matter." For the relative importance of ideological complexion of government, the interest group system, and the independence of central banks see Pierson, "Fragmented Welfare States"; Keman, "Federalism and Policy Performance," 219; Lancaster and Hicks, "Impact of Federalism and Neo-corporatism," 238; and Sakamoto, *Economic Policy and Performance in Industrial Democracies*. Note that the ideological complexion of government and the system of interest group representation are strongly correlated with the electoral system.

17. Lijphart, *Patterns of Democracy*.

18. Lijphart and Crepaz, "Corporatism and Consensus Democracy in Eighteen Countries."

19. Tsebelis, *Veto Players*. While the veto players model was not developed to explain interest group influence in democratic polities, the theories are similar in key respects; both are designed to explain how institutional design affects governments' ability to change the status quo, and both identify institutions that empower actors with potential

vetoes as the key independent variables. Note, however, that Tsebelis does not cite Immergut's veto-points theory in his introduction of the model in 1995 or the book of that name that followed in 2002. The affinity between institutional veto players and veto points is based on their conceptualization in the literature.

20. While Immergut, *Health Politics,* suggests there may be a qualitative difference between single-party majority executives and coalition executives (26), she consistently characterizes all political systems that empower executives to enact their policy programs without challenge as devoid of veto points.

21. Birchfield and Crepaz's distinction between "collective" and "competitive" veto points; Gerring, Thacker, and Moreno, "Centripetal Theory of Democratic Governance," and Gerring and Thacker's *Centripetal Theory of Democratic Governance.*

22. Persson and Tabellini, *Economic Effects of Constitutions.*

23. Note, however, that this expectation is consistent with Huber, Ragin, and Stephens's early veto points model, discussed in "Social Democracy, Christian Democracy, Constitutional Structure, and the Welfare State," which depicted individual legislators rather than parties as the critical veto points in political systems that use single-member district elections.

24. See Iverson and Soskice, "Electoral Systems," for data and an explanatory model.

25. Chang, Kayser, and Rogowski, "Electoral Systems and Real Prices."

26. Lijphart and Crepaz, "Corporatism and Consensus Democracy."

27. Note that ibid. and Lijphart, *Patterns of Democracy,* link corporatism to most consensual institutions on the executive-legislative dimension, including multi-party systems and multi-party executives, both of which are arguably products of PR elections.

28. See Vail, Hasund, and Drake, *Greening of Agricultural Policies,* for a full discussion of the policy area in comparative perspective. See Moyer and Josling, *Agricultural Policy Reform,* for Europe; and Lowi, *The End of Liberalism,* for discussion of the American case.

29. Pappi and Henning, *Organization of Influence,* 270.

30. Van der Bijl, van Zeijts, and Knickel, "Nitrogen Problems and Current Policies."

31. Given electoral system changes in Italy, Japan, and New Zealand, and the formal adoption of federalism in Belgium in the mid-1990s, the study period was ended in 1995. Therefore Austria and Sweden are not members of the European Union during the study period as they joined the EU only in 1995.

32. See Lijphart, *Democracies, Patterns of Democracy,* for the relationship between majoritarian institutions and minority representation; Powell, *Contemporary Democracies,* for institutions and political violence; Powell, *Elections as Instruments of Democracy,* for the relationship between majoritarian institutions and issue congruence with the media voter; Milner, *Civic Literacy;* and Gordon and Segura, "Cross-National Variation," for the role of institutions in political sophistication.

33. Lijphart, *Thinking About Democracy,* 13.

2. The Vulnerability Thesis

1. This definition of an interest group is used throughout the text. It includes corporations that technically have no members, small groups whose members are known to each other, industry groups that represent federations of employers or employees, and public interest groups that include a large number of relatively inactive members. It does not include potential or latent groups that could be organized based on group identity, e.g., women's groups, environmentalists, etc.

2. See Strøm and Müller, "Parliamentary Democracy," on voter delegation.

3. See Baumgartner and Leech, *Basic Interests,* 152, for a summary of research on interest group activities in the Unites States.

4. Downs, *An Economic Theory of Democracy,* 254; Olson, *Rise and Decline of Nations,* 37; Quatronne and Tverskey, "Contrasting Rational and Psychological Analysis."

5. Kollman, *Outside Lobbying;* for an alternative view see Gerber, *Populist Paradox.*

6. See Lupia, "Shortcuts Versus Encyclopedias"; Lau and Redlawsk, "Advantages and Disadvantages."

7. See Samuels, "Pork Barreling," on politicians' use of campaign contributions in Brazil.

8. Arnold, *Logic of Congressional Action;* Steinmo and Tolbert, "Do Institutions Really Matter?"; and Gerring, Thacker, and Moreno, "Centripetal Theory of Democratic Governance."

9. Baumgartner and Leech, *Basic Interests,* 36–38, 59–61.

10. See Powell, *Elections as Instruments of Democracy,* 10–12; and Schmitter, "Ambiguous Virtues of Accountability," for full discussions of the topic.

11. Strøm's usage of the same term refers to voters' prospective ability to identify potential governments.

12. Arnold, *Logic of Congressional Action.*

13. The adoption of universal health care in France followed this model. While Immergut argues that executive authority allowed the president to impose the policy without the support of the legislature, Arnold's model would characterize the president's actions as outside the normal legislative process.

14. Note, however, that Goodin argues that "omnibus legislation may merely enshrine manipulative agenda-setting on the part of those putting together the package" (340), which questions the efficacy of reliance on restrictive rules alone.

15. Gerring and Thacker refer to these same three institutions as "constitutional." The label "primary" is used here in part because Tsebelis defines institutional veto points as those that derive from constitutions whereas partisan veto points derive from the "political game." Given the dominance of this theory and terminology in the literature the use of "constitutional" to refer to the electoral system may confuse readers.

16. Strøm, "Minority Governments in Parliamentary Democracies," and *Minority Governments and Majority Rule.*

17. Moe and Caldwell, "Institutional Foundations of Democratic Government."

18. Lijphart, *Patterns of Democracy.*

19. The question of whether political competition is candidate-centered, as it is in the United States, or party-centered, as it is in Britain, is a separate one and will be addressed below. Whether voters in SMD elections view elections as an evaluation of the party or the individual politician does not affect their ability to hold individual politicians accountable; accountability is high in either case. Differences between candidate- and party-centered SMD elections speak to who is being held accountable and for what, not the ability of voters to hold politicians accountable.

20. This is the "psychological effect" of single-member competition that links SMD to two-party systems in "Duverger's Law," Duverger, *Political Parties* (1964).

21. This is the "mechanical effect" of single-member district competition that links SMD to two-party systems in "Duverger's Law" (1964).

22. Political systems that use PR to seat the legislature also tend to divide committee chairs proportionately, which also diffuses power and responsibility for policy choice. See Strøm, "Minority Governments in Parliamentary Democracies," and *Patterns of Democracy,* for a full discussion and list of countries with proportional distribution of committee chairs.

23. The single non-transferable vote has also been used in Taiwan, Jordan, and Vanuatu and was recently chosen in Afghanistan (Reynolds, "Curious Case of Afghanistan"). Note that parties may also offer voters a party ticket that ranks candidates within the party list, allowing voters to cast a simple vote for an individual party. This has been the norm in races for the Australian Senate, where approximately 95 percent of voters simply vote for their preferred party ticket.

24. This expectation is consistent with rankings in the literature, and most scholars are content to locate these systems in between SMD and pure PR. See Carey and Shugart, "Incentives to Cultivate a Personal Vote," for a detailed ranking.

25. Shugart and Wattenberg, *Mixed Member Electoral Systems.*

26. Interested readers should note that scholars differentiate mixed-member systems into two groups: mixed-member proportional (MMP) and mixed-member majoritarian (MMM). The PR portion of the ballot determines the ultimate distribution of seat in MMP; the two sides of the ballot determine seats independently under MMM. MMM is expected to make individual representatives and parties more vulnerable than MMP, all else equal.

27. This definition is different from that used by Strøm in *Minority Government and Majority Rule,* where he defines identifiability as voters' ability to identify the parties that could be in government prior to elections. Identifiability as used here is more consistent with "clarity of responsibility" as used by Powell and Whitten in "Cross-National Analysis of Economic Voting."

28. This is the same argument made by Powell and Whitten. Three of the factors that contribute to their "clarity of responsibility" measure reflect whether a single majority party governs alone.

29. Weaver and Rockman, *Do Institutions Matter?*, 27; Scruggs, *Sustaining Abundance.* Note that Chiebub's "Presidentialism, Electoral Identifiability, and Budget

Balances in Democratic Systems" argues that identifiability is always high in presidential systems.

30. Lijphart, *Patterns of Democracy.*

31. I thank Matthew Shugart for this insight.

32. Note, however, that there is disagreement on the identifiability and account-ability of presidential regimes. Some argue that presidents are identifiable (Cheibub, "Presidentialism, Electoral Identifiability, and Budget Balances") and accountable (Samuels and Shugart, "Presidentialism, Elections and Representation"). See also Samuels, "Presidentialism and Accountability."

33. Lijphart, "Patterns of Democracies"; Roller, "Performance of Democracies," 137.

34. Samuels, "Presidentialism and Accountability"; Samuels and Shugart, "Presidentialism, Elections and Representation."

35. The placement of some PR/Parliamentary and Unitary systems is, however, consistent with the differentiated models of Birchfield and Crepaz in "Impact of Constitutional Structures"; Gerring, Thacker, and Moreno in "Centripetal Theory of Democratic Governance"; and Gerring and Thacker in *Centripetal Theory of Democratic Governance.* In addition, the vulnerability continuum is able to locate all other political systems where these two models do not.

3. Evidence from the Environment

1. The PR portion of the ballot does compensate to some extent because it promotes a multi-party system, but the effect is limited to supporting smaller parties that normally govern, with one of the larger parties in coalition. Consequently it is reasonable to expect that German politicians are more vulnerable to interest group demands due to the mixed member system.

2. Birchfield and Crepaz, "Impact of Constitutional Structures."

3. Iverson and Soskice, "Electoral Systems."

4. Olson, *Logic of Collective Action; Rise and Decline of Nations.*

5. Such cases are common in the environmental literature. See Strøm and Swindle, "Political Parties"; Scruggs, *Sustaining Abundance.*

6. Feigenbaum, Samuels, and Weaver, "Innovation, Coordination, and Implementation," 43.

7. Vail, Hasund, and Drake, *Greening of Agricultural Policies.*

8. Only in Sweden has the government empowered a countervailing force (the Consumers Delegation, CD, 1963–1990) in agricultural policy making and price-setting (ibid., 103–108). While Vail Hasund, and Drake, *Greening of Agricultural Policies,* state that the CD was a force for "greening" Swedish agriculture, the authors do not attribute any policy reform to the group, nor do they mention the group in reference to policy change of any type throughout their text devoted to the topic. Instead, the authors locate the impetus for reform in other actors, which will be discussed in detail in chapter eight. The absence of discussion on the CD in the text suggests that others

are likely correct in their assessment that the CD did not curb the power of agricultural interests, nor was it a force for policy change.

9. According to the European Environment Agency, as much as 95 percent of the pesticides applied to crops also fail to reach their target pest (*Environment in the European Union at the Turn of the Century,* 116).

10. McGinn, "Promoting Sustainable Fisheries."

11. van der Bijl, "Nitrogen Problems," 7.

12. See European Environment Agency, *Environment in the European Union at the Turn of the Century,* 175, for human health effects of nitrate in water.

13. Ironically, the eradication of a target pest is almost never complete, leaving those most resistant to survive, reproduce, and generate pesticide-resistant strains. As a result, pesticide resistance alters the characteristics of the target population and generates the need for a new pesticide, and the process starts all over again.

14. Swan et al., "Geographic differences"; Hancock et al., "Pesticide Exposure"; Brouchard, Bellinger, Wright, and Weisskopf, "Attention-Deficit/Hyperactivity Disorder."

15. Quoted in van der Bijl, van Zeijts, and Knickel, "Nitrogen Problems," 8.

16. Bernson, *Experiences and Reflections;* Bernson and Ekström, "Swedish Policy to Reduce Pesticide Use"; Emmerman, *Programme to Reduce the Risks,* 6; Pettersson, "Pesticide Use in Swedish Agriculture," 95.

17. Bergkvist, *Pesticide Risk Indicators.*

18. It is also common practice in the institutional literature to separate these "semi-proportional" systems from all other electoral systems.

19. Germany uses a mixed-member system, which increases accountability for those politicians elected by SMD, equaling approximately half the members of legislature. The index ranking of Finland increases by one because it uses an open-list electoral formula. Finland also directly elects a president, but given the weak position of the president no change in index position is made here. Italy's position shifts the same amount because it too utilized an open list before 1995, albeit with multiple votes. Experts also note that many policies are made in legislative committees rather than in plenary session in Italy, which should enhance identifiability for policy choice further, yet no shift in index placement is made here. As noted above, Italy's position is limited to prior to its electoral system change.

20. New Zealand also experienced electoral system change effective in 1996, also demanding a significant shift in ranking after that year.

21. Vogel, *National Styles of Regulation,* 99; Rootes, "Britain," 5; Scruggs, *Sustaining Abundance.*

22. Total input use is not a perfect measure because land use changes over time. Input use per hectare is less imperfect but it does include forested land and it does not allow differentiation of land based on the type of crop grown. Nevertheless, it is used here as it is the best measure available and the standard measure used for cross-national comparisons of agriculture in the literature.

23. Pesticide data for countries includes one figure for 1975 and then usually annual figures for 1980 through 1995.

24. We cannot compare the use of specific chemicals on specific crops because crop-specific data is not collected. Expert advice indicated that the five crops identified are the ones grown in such quantity that changes in land use devoted to their production may generate observable differences in national aggregate agrochemical use (personal interview with Miles Thomas of the Central Science Laboratory in Britain).

25. Examination of the raw data on each variable verifies this expectation, except in the case of nitrogen use in New Zealand. Given the dramatic increase in use in the early 1990s, New Zealand's data on nitrogen use has been adjusted downward for this analysis. Given New Zealand's index value, the adjustment makes it more difficult to substantiate the theory.

26. There are essentially two types of support: the first resulting from a variety of instruments that support market prices, the second from direct subsidies to agriculture that do not affect commodity prices. The PSE includes both types.

27. The income question is that it asks respondents to agree to contribute *more* income, which may illicit "disagree" responses from both the poor and those who already contribute at high levels. The question of whether or not government should protect the environment without raising taxes is subject to the same biases; some respondents may believe they cannot afford new taxes, others may believe the government is doing an adequate job with existing taxes. It would be unreasonable to expect voters to prefer additional government spending in states where government funds or policies already protect the environment effectively. The question regarding others' overstatement of environmental problems may reflect country-specific factors, e.g., whether or not there are Green Parties or vocal environmental groups, and it may increase "agree" responses among respondents in adversarial, i.e., two-party political systems, if environmentalism is "owned" by one party.

28. As expected, an F test confirmed that we could not reject the null hypothesis that the intercepts for the dummies were all simultaneously zero. Therefore, I do not include the dummies as independent variables.

29. The 1985 volume provides data dating back to 1970.

4. The European Union

1. Scheierling, *Overcoming Agricultural Pollution of Water*; Grant, *Common Agricultural Policy* (1997).

2. Winter, *Rural Politics*, 140.

3. McCormick, *European Union*; Tracy, *Agriculture Policy in the European Union*.

4. Ibid., 6.

5. Both areas now suffer severe environmental pollution due to the high quantity of unused animal waste at the ports where water supplies are most vulnerable to nitrates, and throughout inland areas, where water tables are contaminated by the high use of synthetic chemical fertilizers.

6. van der Bijl, van Zeijts, and Knickel, "Nitrogen Problems," 6.

7. The Drinking Water Directive sets maximum levels for a variety of pollutants, including pesticides and fertilizers. Only agrochemicals are considered in this section.

8. Rillearts, personal interview.

9. Quoted in Scheierling, *Overcoming Agricultural Pollution of Water.*

10. Tracy, *Agriculture Policy in the European Union,* 92; Grant, *Common Agricultural Policy,* 77–79.

11. van der Bijl, van Zeijts, and Knickel, "Nitrogen Problems," 14–15.

12. Liefferink, Lowe and Mol, *European Integration and Environmental Policy.*

13. Scheierling, *Overcoming Agricultural Pollution of Water,* 18, for the Community of 12; Anderson and Liefferink, *European Environmental Policy,* for the three later entrants.

5. The United Kingdom

1. The hung parliament and subsequent coalition government of 2010 is a rare exception to that rule.

2. McCormick, *European Union,* 242.

3. Winter, *Rural Politics,* 116.

4. Ibid., 223.

5. Ibid., 232.

6. Central Water Planning Unit, *Nitrate and Water Resources.*

7. Hill, Aaronovitch, and Baldock, "Non-decision Making in Pollution Control," 229.

8. Winter, *Rural Politics,* 269.

9. Ibid., 271.

10. Ibid., 270.

11. The process of designating NVZs was described to me during a personal interview with Fletcher. Unless otherwise indicated, all details of that process on the following pages are a product of that interview.

12. Goldsworthy, personal interview; Davis, personal interview.

13. Ibid.

14. European Commission, *Report to the European Parliament.*

15. Powick, Williamson, and Zamen, personal interview.

16. For the argument that this is in fact a positive characteristic of British politics, see Moe and Caldwell, "Institutional Foundations," 171–195.

17. The Polluter Pays Principle, i.e., that polluters rather than the general public pay the costs of pollution, is one of the fundamental principles of environmental protection. It was formally adopted by the EU, and thus the U.K., with the 1987 Single European Act (SEA).

18. Goldsworthy, personal interview.

19. Winter, *Rural Politics,* 239.

20. Chamberlain, personal interview.

21. Wise, personal interview.

22. Curtoys, personal interview.

23. Chamberlain, personal interview.

24. Thomas, personal interview. Note that the Central Science Laboratory became "Fera," the Food and Environment Research Agency, effective April 1, 2009.

25. As will be discussed in the Swedish case study, another reason rates can be reduced is because manufacturers' "efficacy" is defined by the number of pests remaining after use, which does not necessarily equate to the optimal reduction of pests in terms of yields.

26. Winter, *Rural Politics,* 239.

27. Curtoys, personal interview; Goldsworthy, personal interview; Hards, personal interview; Powick, Williamson, and Zamen, personal interview; Wise, personal interview.

28. Hards, personal interview.

29. Winter, *Rural Politics,* 240–243.

30. Goldsworthy, personal interview.

31. Chamberlain, personal interview.

32. Wise, personal interview.

33. Chamberlain, personal interview.

34. Curtoys, personal interview.

35. Heath *et al.* (1990); Young (1987, 1989) (also cited in Rootes [1995]).

36. Parkin (1989) 223.

37. Rootes, "Britain: Greens in a Cold Climate," 68–69.

38. Frankland (1990) 13.

39. Rootes, "Britain: Greens in a Cold Climate," 81.

40. Ibid., 73.

6. Germany

1. Of the longtime members of the EU, only France, Britain, and Germany are comparable in this policy area. As France also uses single-member district elections (majority-plurality) and is unitary, it does not offer variance on critical variables.

2. From 1949 until 1957, additional small parties were included in government. Between December 1966 and October 1969, the two large parties governed together in a grand coalition.

3. Members of the Bundesrat are not directly elected and do not technically represent the people of an individual *Land.* They are appointed members of Land governments and represent the interests of the Land governments.

4. Conradt, *German Polity,* 193.

5. Federal Environment Agency, *Sustainable Development in Germany,* 114.

6. Conradt, *German Polity,* 145.

7. OECD, *Environmental Performance Reviews: Germany,* 153.

8. LAWA is the German acronym for the Working Group on water issues of the Federal States and the Federal Government represented by the Federal Environment Ministry (1995), quoted in Federal Environment Agency, *Sustainable Development in Germany,* 115–116.

9. LAWA in preparation, quoted in ibid., 118.

10. Winje et al. (1991), quoted in ibid.

11. Recall that a peak organization represents other organizations that represent members of some defined group, in this case farmers, at the national level.

12. Hendriks, *Germany and European Integration,* 144. Note that the DBV is typical of the neo-corporatist model of interest group representation that characterizes German politics. The system is highly structured, hierarchical, and institutionalized. This explains the ability of the DBV to unify what is in reality a varied farm population. It has also been credited with the success of the organization in advancing its interests (Dalton, *Politics in Germany,* 259).

13. Ibid., 144.

14. Vorreyer, personal interview.

15. The CDU and CSU are two separate parties but are conventionally treated as a single party because they campaign together, compose one *fraction* in the Bundestag, and always govern in coalition with one another. Most important, they do not compete with one another; the CSU is strictly a Bavarian party and does not contest elections outside of the southern state of Bavaria, and the CDU does not contest elections in Bavaria.

16. The Greens replaced the FDP as the junior partner in coalition with the SPD from 1998 to 2005. That administration marked the first time the Greens participated in a national government. While the German Greens are among the most powerful Green parties in Europe, it should be noted at the outset that agriculture is not one of the issues that elevated the Green party to its current prominence or that drove its agenda. The German Greens initially focused on two major issues: nuclear power and peace. Air pollution is also a salient issue in Germany, given the devastating effects of acid rain on Germany's forests. Since reunification, the party has also taken up social justice and equality issues, leaving little room to attend to the environmental issues associated with agrochemical use. Thus, while the Greens have been a force on Germany's political stage, the party has not been significant to the policy issues at hand.

17. Tracy, *Agriculture Policy,* 84.

18. Lübbe, personal interview.

19. OECD Environment Directorate, *Activities to Reduce Pesticide Risks,* 228–229.

20. Weingarten, *Agri-Environmental Policy in Germany,* 18.

21. Lysimeter investigations determine the rate at which products decompose.

22. Federal Environment Agency, *Sustainable Development in Germany,* 119.

23. Federal Biological Research Centre for Agriculture and Forestry (hereafter BBA), "Overview: Estimating Consequences-Recognizing Effects."

24. Lübbe, personal interview.

25. BBA, "Overview: Estimating Consequences-Recognizing Effects."

26. Schulz, personal interview.

27. BBA, "Overview: Estimating Consequences-Recognizing Effects."

28. Weingarten, *Agri-Environmental Policy in Germany,* 16.

29. Leser, personal interview.

30. Federal Ministry of Food, Agriculture and Forestry (BML), *The New Ordinance on Fertilisations.*

31. Prohibitions are a product of EU legislation. Federal Ministry of Food, Agriculture and Forestry (BML), *The New Ordinance on Fertilisation.*

32. Leser, personal interview, quoted in Weingarten, *Agri-Environmental Policy in Germany,* 18.

33. Leser, personal interview.

34. Eichler and Schulz, "Nitrogen Reduction Programme," 613.

35. Wilson (1994), quoted in Baldock, "Environmental Impacts of Agri-Environmental Measures."

36. Agro-Europe (1996), quoted in Weingarten, *Agri-Environmental Policy in Germany,* 18.

37. Baldock, "Environmental Impacts of Agri-Environmental Measures," 131.

38. Federal Environmental Agency, *Sustainable Development in Germany,* 138.

39. Leser, personal interview.

40. Frangenburg, personal interview.

41. von Krocher, personal interview.

42. Schulz, personal interview.

43. von Krocher, personal interview.

44. Baumgartel, personal interview.

45. The details of the two approaches described are taken from Weingarten, *Agri-Environmental Policy in Germany.*

46. The average rate of compensation paid to farmers in this particular Land during the study period was 310 DM/ha of arable land.

47. Weingarten, *Agri-Environmental Policy in Germany,* 16.

48. Water suppliers have engaged in other activities as well, including purchasing land and repairing sewer leaks, to preclude contamination of water supplies that they would be responsible for cleaning up in the future before delivering the water to customers (Frangenburg, personal interview).

49. The following information is from personal interview with Wolf.

50. Lübbe, personal interview. Lübbe also noted that the use of taxes is expanding. As of 1999, groundwater taxes were used to compensate farmers for reductions in agrochemical use in 13 of the 16 Länder.

51. Wolf, personal interview.

52. Ibid.; Lübbe, personal interview.

53. Schulz, personal interview.

54. Weingarten (1996), quoted in Weingarten, *Agri-Environmental Policy in Germany,* 21–22.

7. Austria

1. Eder, personal interview.

2. Posch, personal interview.

3. Baumhofer, personal interview.

4. Posch, personal interview.

5. Prior to 1995, when Austria became a member of the European Union and therefore a beneficiary of CAP subsidies based on production.

6. Eder, personal interview.

7. Molterer, *Making Growth in Organic Trade a Priority,* 1–2.

8. Ibid., 2.

9. Ibid., 3.

10. Federal Ministry of Agriculture and Forestry, *Promotion of Organic ("Biological") Farming in Austria.*

11. Molterer, *Making Growth in Organic Trade a Priority,* 3.

12. Ibid.

13. Posch, personal interview.

14. Anticipation of an "over-supply" has since proven to be correct. Two-thirds of the milk produced organically, for example, is sold as conventional due to the lack of a market.

15. Molterer, *Making Growth in Organic Trade a Priority,* 4.

16. ÖPUL (Austrian Program for Environmental Agriculture), *Overview of National and Regional Support Policies,* 19.

17. Ibid., 35.

18. The shift from conventional farming to organic farming tends to reduce yields dramatically the first year, but less so in subsequent years, until levels of production can sometimes be equalized by the seventh year. In areas less favorable for farming, however, organic production will never attain the yields of conventional methods. Importantly, farmers are generally not able to market their products as "organic" unless the land has been farmed according to strict standards for at least five years, precluding the opportunity for higher prices normally associated with organics.

19. Federal Ministry of Agriculture and Forestry, *Promotion of Organic ("Biological") Farming in Austria.*

20. ÖPUL, *Overview of National and Regional Support Policies,* 20.

21. Molterer, *Making Growth in Organic Trade a Priority,* 7.

22. Membership in the EU does not preclude the use of economic instruments; Denmark instituted agrochemical charges and it has been a member of the EU as long as Britain.

23. Schwaiger, personal interview.

24. OECD, *Environmental Performance Reviews: Austria,* 58.

25. Eder, personal interview.

26. Posch, personal interview. Note that Austrian farms are small compared to Britain's and Germany's farms, averaging only 10–30 hectares in size. The term "large" as used here is relative to other farms in Austria.

27. Ibid.

28. Federal Ministry of Agriculture and Forestry, *Promotion of Organic ("Biological") farming in Austria,* 1.

29. Lauber, "Austria: A Latecomer Which Became a Pioneer," 83.

30. See ibid., 100–114, for an excellent account of policy shifts on these and other issues.

31. Ibid.

32. Ibid., 92, 97.

33. To tax nutrient surpluses governments must sample soils on every farm before and after harvest to determine if more fertilizers were used than the crop could use. While imposing costs only on true polluters, this is a labor-intensive and technologically expensive policy option.

8. Sweden

1. According to Vail, Hasund, and Drake, a consumers' group (Consumers Delegation—CD) was formally included in agricultural policy making from 1963 to 1990. The influence of that group is unfortunately unclear, as it is not mentioned by the authors in conjunction with any specific aspect of the "greening" of Swedish agricultural policy in their book on that topic. Other authors have argued that the CD was a rubber-stamp for policies decided by agricultural interests, citing the fact that the CD was primarily involved in price negotiations and that Swedish food prices remained much higher than world levels throughout their tenure. Notably, the CD was not mentioned by any group interviewed by the author with respect to any aspect of policy choice, agrochemical-environmental or otherwise, and is therefore not discussed here. For a full account of the CD and for citations from the Swedish-language literature see Vail, Hasund, and Drake, *Greening of Agricultural Policies,* 103–108.

2. Federation of Swedish Farmers, *Swedish Farmers and Their Companies,* 5.

3. Vail, Hasund, and Drake, *Greening of Agricultural Policies,* 11.

4. Ibid., 67–70.

5. Ibid., 126.

6. Ibid., 77.

7. Ibid., 12.

8. Ibid., 144.

9. Emmerman, *Programme to Reduce Risks* (1992), 10.

10. Ekström and Bernson, "Swedish Pesticide Policies 1972–93," 42.

11. Ibid., 43.

12. Vail, Hasund, and Drake, *Greening of Agricultural Policies,* 144.

13. Eksvard, Persson, and Sandrup, personal interview.

14. Vail, Hasund, and Drake, *Greening of Agricultural Policies,* 145.

15. The Swedish Board of Agriculture is similar to the Agriculture Department in the United States; it is the government authority in agriculture and is responsible for rural development programs, animal welfare, crop production, marketing, etc.

16. Ekström and Bernson, "Swedish Pesticide Policies 1972–93," 44.

17. Vail, Hasund, and Drake, *Greening of Agricultural Policies,* 159.

18. Eksvard, Persson, and Sandrup, personal interview.

19. The National Chemicals Inspectorate (KemI) is a supervisory agency, part of the Ministry of the Environment, responsible for supervising manufacturers and importers of chemicals and pesticide registration.

20. Emmerman, *Programme to Reduce Risks* (1997), 3; Pettersson, "Pesticide Use in Swedish Agriculture," 94.

21. Ekström and Bernson, "Swedish Pesticide Policies 1972–93."

22. Löfstedt, "Swedish Chemical Regulation," 414.

23. Pettersson, "Pesticide Use in Swedish Agriculture," 93; Bellinder, Gummessorn, and Karlsson, "Percentage-Driven Government Mandates for Pesticide Reduction," 355.

24. Emmerman, *Programme to Reduce Risks* (1997), 13. The "substitution principle" will be discussed at length later in the chapter. It denies approval of pesticides that pose a greater risk to the environment than do alternative products that can perform the same function.

25. Bergkvist, *Pesticide Risk Indicators.*

26. Bernson and Ekström, "Swedish Policy to Reduce Pesticide Use," 34.

27. Vail, Hasund, and Drake, *Greening of Agricultural Policies,* 158.

28. Bernson, *Swedish Risk Reduction Programmes,* 1–2; Emmerman, *Programme to Reduce Risks* (1992).

29. Pettersson, "Pesticide Use in Swedish Agriculture," 100.

30. Bernson, *Experiences and Reflections.*

31. Bergkvist, Bernson, Jarl, and Törnlund, "Re-registration of Pesticides in Sweden," 12; Emmerman, *Programme to Reduce Risks* (1997), 5.

32. Bernson, *Swedish Risk Reduction Programmes,* 4.

33. Ibid., 5.

34. Ibid.

35. Ibid.

36. Ljunggren, personal interview.

37. Pettersson, "Pesticide Use in Swedish Agriculture," 85.

38. Johansson, Paulsson, and Nibleaus (1986), quoted in Bellinder, Gummessorn, and Karlsson, "Percentage-Driven Government Mandates," 352.

39. Ibid.

40. Emmerman, *Programme to Reduce Risks* (1992).

41. Vail, Hasund, and Drake, *Greening of Agricultural Policies,* 140.

42. Bellinder, Gummessorn, and Karlsson, "Percentage-Driven Government Mandates," 352.

43. Bernson, *Experiences and Reflections.*

44. Vail, Hasund, and Drake, *Greening of Agricultural Policies,* 158.

45. Bernson, *Experiences and Reflections;* Bernson and Ekström, "Swedish Policy to Reduce Pesticide Use"; Emmerman *Programme to Reduce Risks* (1997), 6; Pettersson, "Pesticide Use in Swedish Agriculture," 95.

46. Emmerman, *Programme to Reduce Risks* (1992), 9.

47. Emmerman, *Programme to Reduce Risks* (1997), 5.

48. Johansson, Paulsson, and Nibleaus (1986), cited by Bellinder, Gummessorn, and Karlsson, "Percentage-Driven Government Mandates," 352; Vail, Hasund, and Drake, *Greening of Agricultural Policies*, 158.

49. Bellinder, Gummessorn, and Karlsson, "Percentage-Driven Government Mandates," 352.

50. Emmerman, *Programme to Reduce Risks* (1992), 9.

51. Emmerman, *Programme to Reduce Risks* (1997), 9; Pettersson, "Pesticide Use in Swedish Agriculture," 97.

52. Bernson, *Swedish Risk Reduction Programmes*, 2.

53. Eksvard, Persson, and Sandrup, personal interview.

54. Vail, Hasund, and Drake, *Greening of Agricultural Policies*, 171–172.

55. Johansson, Paulsson, and Nibleaus (1986), quoted in Bellinder, Gummessorn, and Karlsson, "Percentage-Driven Government Mandates," 353.

56. Bellinder, Gummessorn, and Karlsson, "Percentage-Driven Government Mandates," 353.

57. Bernson, *Experiences and Reflections.*

58. Emmerman, *Programme to Reduce Risks* (1992), 8.

59. Bellinder, Gummessorn, and Karlsson, "Percentage-Driven Government Mandates," 353.

60. Emmerman, *Programme to Reduce Risks* (1999).

61. Emmerman, *Programme to Reduce Risks* (1997).

62. Emmerman, *Programme to Reduce Risks* (1992), 7; Vail, Hasund, and Drake, *Greening of Agricultural Policies*, 158.

63. Emmerman, *Programme to Reduce Risks* (1997), 10.

64. Bernson, *Swedish Risk Reduction Programmes*, 3.

65. Ibid., 2.

66. Ibid., 3.

67. OECD, *Agricultural Policy Reform and Adjustment*, 14.

68. Ljungstrom, personal interview.

69. Bellinder, Gummessorn, and Karlsson, "Percentage-Driven Government Mandates," 358.

70. Vail, Hasund, and Drake, *Greening of Agricultural Policies*, 65.

71. Bellinder, Gummessorn, and Karlsson, "Percentage-Driven Government Mandates," 353. The program costs for KemI, including research, testing, and advisory services were less than 5 million SEK a year (Emmerman, *Programme to Reduce Risks* [1992], 11).

72. Last, but not least, "the net impact on farmers' economy is positive" (ibid.).

73. Vail, Hasund, and Drake, *Greening of Agricultural Policies*, 128.

74. Vail, Hasund, and Drake, *Greening of Agricultural Policies*, 13, 124–129.

75. Bennulf, "Rise and Fall of Miljöpartiet de Gröna,"138.

9. Institutional Design and the Quality of Democracy

1. See Lundqvist, *Hare and the Tortoise;* Fiorina, *Divided Government;* Nelson, Tietenberg, and Donihue, "Differential Environmental Regulation"; and Vogel, *National Styles of Regulation,* 103–104.

2. Porter, Brown, and Chasek, *Global Environmental Politics,* chapter 2.

3. Dai, "Conditional Nature of Democratic Compliance."

4. Immergut, "Institutions, Veto Points, and Policy Results," 411.

5. Steinmo and Watts, "It's the Institutions, Stupid!"

6. Rogowski and Kayser, "Majoritarian Electoral System," link political systems dominated by large parties to low consumer prices; Persson and Tabellini, "Size and Scope of Government," *Economic Effects of Constitutions,* to low government spending.

BIBLIOGRAPHY

Anderson, Mikael Skou, and Duncan Liefferink, eds. 1997. *European Environmental Policy: The Pioneers*. Oxford: Manchester University Press.

Arnold, R. Douglas. 1990. *The Logic of Congressional Action*. New Haven: Yale University Press.

Atkinson, Anthony B., Lee Rainwater, and Timothy M. Smeeding. 1995. *Income Distribution in OECD Countries: Evidence from the Luxembourg Income Study*. Paris: OECD.

Baldock, David. 1996. "Environmental Impacts of Agri-Environmental Measures." *Subsidies and the Environment: Exploring the Linkages*. Paris: OECD.

Baumgartel, Gerhard. May 24, 1999. Personal interview. Agricultural Chamber of Hannover. Hannover.

Baumgartner, Frank R., and Beth L. Leech. 1998. *Basic Interests*. Princeton: Princeton University Press.

Baumhofer, Elizabeth. April 27, 1999. Personal interview. OBV (Mountain farmers organization). Vienna.

Bellinder, Robin R., Gunnar Gummessorn, and Christer Karlsson. 1994. "Percentage-Driven Government Mandates for Pesticide Reduction: The Swedish Model." *Weed Technology* 8:350–359.

Bennulf, Martin. 1995. "The Rise and Fall of Miljöpartiet de Gröna." In *The Green Challenge: The Development of Green Parties in Europe*, ed. Dick Richardson and Chris Rootes. London: Routledge.

Berelson, Bernard. 1952. "Democratic Theory and Public Opinion." *Public Opinion Quarterly* 16:313–330.

Bergkvist, Peter. 1997. *Pesticide Risk Indicators Used in Sweden*. Solna: National Chemicals Inspectorate.

Bergkvist, Peter, Vibeke Bernson, Sylvia Jarl, and Monica Törnlund. 1996. "Re-registration of Pesticides in Sweden—Results from the Review 1990–1995." *Pesticide Outlook* (December):12–18.

Bernhard, William, and David LeBlang. 1999. "Democratic Institutions and Exchange-rate Commitments." *International Organization* 53 (1):71–97.

Bernson, Vibeke. 1989. "Experiences and Reflections on Registration and Reregistration of Pesticides." Seminar on Pesticides in Agriculture presented at EC-EFTA Meeting, University of Agricultural Sciences, Uppsala, November 14–15.

———. 1993. "The Role of Science in Pesticide Management—An International Comparison: The Swedish Experience." *Regulatory Toxicology and Pharmacology* 17:249–261.

———. 1995. *Will Regulatory Pressure Eliminate the Need for New Herbicides?* Weeds: Brighton Crop Protection Conference.

———. 1997. *The Swedish Risk Reduction Programmes for Pesticides, Results and Enforcements.* Brussels: Colloquium: Mogelijkheden European ervaringen met nationale pesticiden-reductieprogramma's in de context van de Europese Unie, April 11.

Bernson, Vibeke, and George Ekström. 1991. "Swedish Policy to Reduce Pesticide Use." *Pesticide Outlook* 2 (3):33–36.

Birchfield, Vicki, and Marcus Crepaz. 1998. "The Impact of Constitutional Structures and Collective and Competitive Veto Points on Income Inequality in Industrialized Democracies." *European Journal of Political Research* 34:175–200.

Bostrom, Ann, et al. 1994. "What Do People Know About Climate Change? 1. Mental Models." *Risk Analysis* 14 (6):959–969.

Brouchard, Maryse F., David C. Bellinger, Robert O. Wright, and Marc G. Weisskopf, "Attention-Deficit/Hyperactivity Disorder and Urinary Metabolites of Organophoshate Pesticides." *Pediatrics* (2010).

Bueno de Mesquita, Bruce, Alastair Smith, Randolph M. Siverson, and James D. Morrow. 2003. *The Logic of Political Survival.* Cambridge, Mass.: MIT Press.

Cain, Bruce, John Ferejohn, and Morris P. Fiorina. 1987. *The Personal Vote: Constituency Service and Electoral Independence.* Cambridge: Cambridge University Press.

Cameron, David. R. 1978. "The Expansion of the Public Economy: A Comparative Analysis." *The American Political Science Review* 72 (4):1243–1261.

Carey, John, and Matthew S. Shugart. 1995. "Incentives to Cultivate a Personal Vote: A Rank Ordering of Electoral Formulas." *Electoral Studies* 14:417–439.

Castles, F. G., and R. McKinlay. 1979. "Does Politics Matter? An Analysis of the Public Welfare Commitment in Advanced Democratic States." *European Journal of Political Research* 7:169–186.

Central Water Planning Unit. 1977. *Nitrate and Water Resources with Particular Reference to Groundwater.* Reading: Central Water Planning Unit.

Chamberlain, Philip. March 6, 1999. Personal interview. Crowmarsh Battle Farm. Wallingford, England.

Cheibub, José Antonio. 2006 "Presidentialism, Electoral Identifiability, and Budget Balances in Democratic Systems." *American Political Science Review* 100 (3).

Choplin, Gerald. February 4, 1999. Personal interview. CPE Farmers Union. Brussels.

Codd. March 1, 1999. Personal interview. Highfield Farm. Bedfordshire, England.

Committee on Political Parties, American Political Science Association. 1950. "Toward a More Responsible Two-Party System." *American Political Science Review* 44, supplement.

Committee on the Environment, Public Health and Consumer Protection. 1998. *Environmental Taxes and Charges in the Single Market.* Brussels: European Commission.

Congleton, Roger D. 1992. "Political Institutions and Pollution Control." *Review of Economics and Statistics.* 412–421.

Conradt, David P. 1996. *The German Polity.* White Plains: Longman.

Cox, Gary W. 1987. *The Efficient Secret: The Cabinet and the Development of Political Parties in Victorian England.* Cambridge: Cambridge University Press.

———. 1997. *Making Votes Count: Strategic Coordination in the World's Electoral Systems.* New York: Cambridge University Press.

Cox, Gary W., and Samuel Kernell, eds. 1991. *The Politics of Divided Government.* Boulder: Westview Press.

Cox, Gary W., and Mathew D. McCubbins. 2001. "The Institutional Determinants of Economic Policy Outcomes." In *Presidents, Parliaments, and Policy,* ed. Stephan Haggard and Mathew D. McCubbins. New York: Cambridge University Press.

Crepaz, Marcus M. L. 1998. "Inclusion Versus Exclusion: Political Institutions and Welfare Expenditures." *Comparative Politics.* 61–80.

Crepaz, Marcus M. L., and Ann W. Moser. 2004. "The Impact of Collective and Competitive Veto Points on Public Expenditures in the Global Age." *Comparative Political Studies* 37 (3):259–285.

Curtoys, Jonathan. 1999. Personal interview. Royal Society for the Protection of Birds. Bedfordshire, United Kingdom.

Dahl, Robert. 1961. *Who Governs: Democracy and Power in an American City.* New Haven: Yale University Press.

Dai, Xinyuan. 2006. "The Conditional Nature of Democratic Compliance." *Journal of Conflict Resolution* 50 (5):690–713.

Dalton, Russell J. 1993. *Politics in Germany.* New York: Harper Collins.

Davis, Tim J. March 4, 1999. Personal interview. Head of Environment and Residues Policy Branch, Pesticides Safety Directorate within the Ministry of Agriculture, Fisheries and Food. York, United Kingdom.

DeBois, Marc. May 28, 1999. Personal interview. Environment Directorate, European Commission. Brussels.

Department of the Environment. 1988. *The Nitrate Issue: A Study of the Economic and Other Consequences of Various Local Options for Limiting Nitrate Concentrations in Drinking Water.* London: Department of the Environment.

Dimock, Michael. 1995. "Political Knowledge and Partisanship: The Salience of Cues in American Politics." Ph.D. diss., University of California, San Diego.

Dinan, Desmond. 1999. *Ever Closer Union.* Boulder: Lynne Rienner.

Douthwaite, Nicholas C. 1999. Personal interview. Senior Agricultural Advisor, European Fertilizer Manufacturers Association. Brussels.

Downs, Anthony. 1957. *An Economic Theory of Democracy.* New York: HarperCollins.
Drinking Water Inspectorate. 1998. *Drinking Water 1997.* Cardiff: Department of the Environment, Transport and the Regions.
Duverger, Maurice. 1964. *Political Parties: Their Organization and Activity in the Modern State.* 3d ed. London: Methuen.
Eder, Helmut. April 27, 1999. Personal interview. Agricultural Chamber. Vienna.
Eichler, Franziska, and Dietrich Schulz. 1998. "The Nitrogen Reduction Programme in the Federal Republic of Germany." *Environmental Pollution* 102:609–617.
Ekström, George. 1992. *Pesticide Risk Reduction: The Swedish Example.* Menlo Park, Calif.: PANNA Regional Conference. October 18–20.
Ekström, George, and Vibeke Bernson. 1995. "Swedish Pesticide Policies 1972–93: Risk Reduction and Environmental Charges." *Reviews of Environmental Contamination and Toxicology* 41:27–69.
Ekström, George, Helena Hemming, and Margareta Pamborg. 1996. "Swedish Pesticide Risk Reduction 1981–1995: Food Residues, Health Hazard, and Reported Poisonings." *Reviews of Environmental Contamination and Toxicology* 47: 119–147.
Eksvard, Jan, Soren Persson, and Alarik Sandrup. June 7, 1999. Personal interview. Federation of Swedish Farmers. Stockholm.
Emmerman, Anders. 1992. *Programme to Reduce the Risks Connected with the Use of Pesticides in Sweden.* Jönköping: Swedish Board of Agriculture.
———. 1997. *Programme to Reduce the Risks Connected with the Use of Pesticides— Swedish Experiences.* Jönköping: Swedish Board of Agriculture.
———. 1999. *Programme to Reduce the Risks Connected with the Use of Pesticides in Sweden.* Jönköping: Swedish Board of Agriculture.
Eriksson, Rolf. May 20, 1999. Personal interview. Federation of Swedish Farmers. Brussels.
Esping-Anderson, Gøsta. 1980. *The Three Worlds of Welfare Capitalism.* Princeton: Princeton University Press.
European Commission. 1997. *Report to the European Parliament and to the Council on the Application of Council Regulation (EEC) No. 2078/92.* Brussels.
———. 1998. *Measures Taken Pursuant to Council Directive 91/676/EEC Concerning the Protection of Waters Against Pollution Caused by Nitrates from Agricultural Sources.* Brussels.
European Environment Agency. 1992. *Europe's Environment: The Dobris Assessment.* Copenhagen.
———. 1999. *Environment in the European Union at the Turn of the Century.* Copenhagen.
Federal Biological Research Centre for Agriculture and Forestry (BBA). 1999. "Overview: Estimating Consequences-Recognizing Effects." http://www.bba.de/ english/overview/overview.htm.
Federal Environment Agency. 1998. *Sustainable Development in Germany: Progress and Prospects.* Berlin: Umweltbundesamt.

Federal Law Gazette for the Republic of Austria. 1997. *Plant Protection Products Act 1997*. Vienna: Federal Ministry of Agriculture and Forestry.

Federal Ministry of Agriculture and Forestry. 1997. *Promotion of Organic ("Biological") Farming in Austria*. (Internal document.) Vienna: Federal Ministry of Agriculture and Forestry.

————. 1998. *Organic Farming in Austria*. Vienna: Federal Ministry of Agriculture and Forestry.

Federal Ministry of Food, Agriculture and Forestry (BML). 1996. *The New Ordinance on Fertilisation*. Bonn: BML.

Federation of Swedish Farmers (LRF). 1995. *Swedish Farmers and Their Companies*. Stockholm: LRF.

Feigenbaum, Harvey, Richard Samuels, and R. Kent Weaver. 1993. "Innovation, Coordination, and Implementation in Energy Policy." In *Do Institutions Matter? Government Capabilities in the United States and Abroad*, ed. R. Kent Weaver and Bert A. Rockman, 42–109. Washington D.C.: Brookings Institution.

Finer, S. E., ed. 1975. *Adversary Politics and Electoral Reform*. London: William Clowes & Sons.

Fiorina, Morris. 1992. *Divided Government*. New York: Macmillan.

Fiorino, Daniel J. 1995. *Making Environmental Policy*. Berkeley and Los Angeles: University of California Press.

Fletcher, Steve. March 1, 1999. Personal interview. The Groundwater Protection Center, U.K. Environment Agency. West Midlands, United Kingdom.

Frangenberg, Andreas. May 17, 1999. Personal Interview. Society for the Promotion of Integrated Crop Production (FIP). Bonn.

Frankland, Erich G. 1990. "Does Green Politics Have a Future in Britain?" In *Green Politics One*, ed. W. Rüdig, 7–28. Edinburgh: Edinburgh University Press.

Gerber, Elisabeth R. 1999. *The Populist Paradox: Interest Group Influence and the Promise of Direct Legislation*. Princeton: Princeton University Press.

Gerring, John, and Strom C. Thacker. 2008. *A Centripetal Theory of Democratic Governance*. Cambridge: Cambridge University Press.

Gerring, John, Strom C. Thacker, and Carola Moreno. 2005. "A Centripetal Theory of Democratic Governance." *American Political Science Review* 99 (4):567–581.

Geyer-Allely, Elaine. 1994. "Agriculture and the Environment in the Transition to a Market Economy." In *Agriculture, Technology and the Environment in OECD Member Countries*. Paris: OECD.

Goldsworthy, Patrick. March 1, 1999. Personal interview. British Agrochemicals Association (BAA). Peterborough, United Kingdom.

Goodin, Robert E. 1996. "Institutionalizing the Public Interest: The Defense of Deadlock and Beyond." *American Political Science Review* 90 (2):331–343.

Gordon, Stacy B., and Gary M. Segura. 1997. "Cross-National Variation in the Political Sophistication of Individuals: Capability or Choice? *Journal of Politics* 59 (1):126–147.

Granberg, Donald, and Soren Holmberg. 1990. "The Berelson Paradox Reconsidered." *Public Opinion Quarterly* 54:530–550.

Grant, Wyn. 1997. *The Common Agricultural Policy*. London: Macmillan.

Gunther, Richard, and Anthony Mughan. 1993. "Political Institutions and Cleavage Management." In *Do Institutions Matter? Government Capabilities in the United States and Abroad*, ed. R. Kent Weaver and Bert A. Rockman, 288. Washington D.C.: Brookings Institution.

Gustavsson, Jan. 1999. *Integration of Environmental Concerns into Agricultural Policy in Sweden*. Jönköping: Swedish Board of Agriculture.

Hammel, Michael. March 26, 1999. Personal interview. Environment Directorate, Commission of the European Union. Brussels.

Hancock, Dana B., Eden R Martin, Gregory M. Mayhew, Jeffrey M. Stajich, Rita Jewett, Mark A. Stacy, Burton L. Scott, Jeffery M. Vance, and William K. Scott. 2008. "Pesticide Exposure and Risk of Parkinson's Disease: A Family-based Case-control Study." *BMC Neurology* 8:6. http://www.biomedcentral.com/1471-2377/8/6.

Hardin, Garrett. 1968. "The Tragedy of the Commons." *Science* 162 (3859): 1243–1248.

Hardin, Russell. 1982. *Collective Action*. Baltimore: Johns Hopkins University Press.

Hards, Justine J. 1999. Personal interview. Linking Environmental and Farming. Warwickshire, United Kingdom.

Heath, Anthony, Roger Jowell, John Curtice, and Geoff Evans. 1990. "The Rise of the New Political Agenda?" *European Sociological Review* 6 (1):31–48.

Heclo, Hugh, and Henrik Madsen. 1987. *Policy and Politics in Sweden: Principled Pragmatism*. Philadelphia: Temple University Press.

Hendriks, Gisela. 1991. *Germany and European Integration: The Common Agricultural Policy—An Area of Conflict*. Oxford: Berg.

Hill, M., S. Aaronovitch, and David Baldock. 1989. "Non-decision Making in Pollution Control in Britain: Nitrate Pollution, the EEC Drinking Water Directive and Agriculture." *Policy and Politics* (17) 3:227–240.

Hix, Simon. 1998. "The Study of the European Union II: The 'New governance' Agenda and Its Rival." *Journal of European Public Policy* 5:1, 38–65.

Hoevenagel, Ruud, Edwin van Noort, and Rene de Kok. 1999. *Study on a European Union Wide Regulatory Framework for Levies on Pesticides*. Zoetermeer: EIM/Haskoning.

House of Lords Select Committee on the European Communities. 1989. *Nitrate in Water*. London: Her Majesty's Stationery Office.

Huber, Evelyn, Charles Ragin, and John D. Stephens. 1993. "Social Democracy, Christian Democracy, Constitutional Structure, and the Welfare State." *American Journal of Sociology* 99:711–749.

Immergut, Ellen. 1990. "Institutions, Veto Points and Policy Results: A Comparative Analysis of Health Care." *Journal of Public Policy* 10 (4).

———. 1992. *Health Politics: Interests and Institutions in Western Europe*. New York: Cambridge University Press.

Inglehart, Ronald. 1995. "Public Support for Environmental Protection: The Impact of Objective Problems and Subjective Values in 43 Societies." *Political Science & Politics* 28 (March):57–72.

Iversen, Torben, and David Soskice. 2006. "Electoral Systems and the Politics of Coalitions: Why Some Democracies Redistribute More Than Others." *American Political Science Review* 100 (2):165–181.

Jordan, Andrew. March 3, 1999. Personal interview. CSERGE, School of Environmental Sciences, University of East Anglia. Norwich.

Katzenstein, Peter J. 1984. *Corporatism and Change: Austrian, Switzerland and the Politics of Industry.* Ithaca, N.Y.: Cornell University Press.

Keman, Hans. 2000. "Federalism and Policy Performance: A Conceptual and Empirical Inquiry." In *Federalism and Political Performance,* ed. Ute Wachendorfer-Schmidt. New York: Routledge.

Kempton, Willett. 1997. "How the Public Views Climate Change." *Environment* 39:12–21.

Kollman, Ken. 1998. *Outside Lobbying: Public Opinion and Interest Group Strategies.* Princeton: Princeton University Press.

Kraft, Michael E., and Norman J. Vig. 1994. "Environmental Policy from the 1970s to the 1990s: Continuity and Change." In *Environmental Policy in the 1990s,* ed. Norman J. Vig and Michael E. Kraft. 2d ed. Washington, D.C.: CQ Press.

Krehbiel, Keith, 1991. *Information and Legislative Organization.* Ann Arbor: University of Michigan Press.

Kronsell, Annica. 1997. "Sweden: Setting a Good Example." In *European Environmental Policy: The Pioneers,* ed. Mikael Skou Anderson and Duncan Liefferink. Oxford: Manchester University Press.

Lancaster, Thomas D., and Alexander M. Hicks. 2000. "The Impact of Federalism and Neo-corporatism on Economic Performance—An Analysis of 18 OECD Countries." In *Federalism and Political Performance,* ed. Ute Wachendorfer-Schmidt. New York: Routledge.

Lau, Richard R., and David P. Redlawsk. 2001. "Advantages and Disadvantages of Cognitive Heuristics in Political Decision Making." *American Journal of Political Science* 45 (4):951–971.

Lauber, Volkmar. 1997. "Austria: A Latecomer Which Became a Pioneer." In *European Environmental Policy: The Pioneers,* ed. Mikael Skou Anderson and Duncan Liefferink. Oxford: Manchester University Press.

Legg, Wilfrid. 1994. "Agriculture Policy Reform and the Environment in OECD Countries." In *Agriculture and the Environment in the Transition to a Market Economy.* Paris: OECD.

Leser, Hans. May 17, 1999. Personal interview. German Farmers Union. Bonn.

Liefferink, J. D., P. D. Lowe, and A. P. J. Mol, eds. 1993. *European Integration and Environmental Policy.* London: Belhaven Press.

Lijphart, Arend. 1984. *Democracies: Patterns of Majoritarian and Consensus Government in Twenty-One Countries.* New Haven: Yale University Press.

———. 1991. "Constitutional Choices for New Democracies." *Journal of Democracy* 2 (1):72–84.

————. 1994. *Electoral Systems and Party Systems: A Study of Twenty-Seven Democracies, 1945–1990*. Oxford: Oxford University Press.

————. 1999. *Patterns of Democracy: Government Forms and Performance in Thirty-Six Countries*. New Haven: Yale University Press.

————. 2008. *Thinking About Democracy: Power Sharing and Majority Rule in Theory and Practice*. New York: Routledge.

Lijphart, Arend, and Markus M. L. Crepaz. 1991. "Corporatism and Consensus Democracy in Eighteen Countries: Conceptual and Empirical Linkages." *British Journal of Political Science* 21 (2):235–246.

Lijphart, Arend, Ronald Rogowski, and R. Kent Weaver. 1993. "Separation of Powers and Cleavage Management." In *Do Institutions Matter? Government Capabilities in the United States and Abroad*, ed. R. Kent Weaver and Bert A. Rockman, 302–344. Washington D.C.: Brookings Institution.

Linz, Juan. 1990. "The Perils of Presidentialism." *Journal of Democracy* 1:51–69.

Ljunggren, Cecilia. June 7, 1999. Personal interview. Director, Association of Swedish Plant and Wood Protection Industries. Stockholm.

Ljungstrom, Krister. June 8, 1999. Personal interview. Swedish Environmental Protection Agency. Stockholm.

Löfstedt, Ragnar E. 2003. "Swedish Chemical Regulation: An Overview and Analysis." *Risk Analysis* 23 (2):411–421.

Lowi, Theodore J. 1969. *The End of Liberalism*. New York: W. W. Norton.

Lübbe, Eiko. May 17, 1999. Personal interview. Ministry of Food, Agriculture and Forestry. Bonn.

Lukschanderl, Leopold. 1992. *Environmental Protection in Austria*. Vienna: Federal Chancellery, Federal Press Service.

Lundqvist, Lennart. 1980. *The Hare and the Tortoise: Clean Air Policies in the United States and Sweden*. Ann Arbor: University of Michigan Press.

Lupia, Arthur. 1994. "Shortcuts Versus Encyclopedias: Information and Voting Behavior in California Insurance Reform Elections." *American Political Science Review* 88:63–76.

Mainwaring, Scott. 1991. "Politicians, Parties, and Electoral Systems: Brazil in Comparative Perspective." *Comparative Politics* (October):21–43.

Mainwaring, Scott, and Matthew S. Shugart, eds. 1998. *Presidentialism and Democracy in Latin America*. Cambridge: Cambridge University Press.

Maioni, Antonia. 1997. "Parting at the Crossroads: The Development of Health Insurance in Canada and United States, 1940–1965." *Comparative Politics* 29 (4):411–432.

Marks, Mike. 1999. Personal interview. Framing and Rural Conservation Agency. London.

Matland, Richard. E., and Donley T. Studlar, 2004. "Determinants of Legislative Turnover: A Cross-National Analysis." *British Journal of Political Science* 34:87–108.

Mayhew, David R. 1974. *Congress: The Electoral Connection*. New Haven: Yale University Press.

Mazur, Allan, and Jinling Lee. 1993. "Sounding the Global Alarm: Environmental Issues in the US National News." *Social Studies of Science* 23:681–720.

McConnell, Grant. 1966. *Private Power and American Democracy.* New York: Alfred A. Knopf.

McCormick, John. 1996. *The European Union: Politics and Policies.* Oxford: Westview Press.

McCubbins, Mathew D., and Talbot Page. 1987. "A Theory of Congressional Delegation." In *Structure and Policy,* ed. Mathew McCubbins and Terry Sullivan. Cambridge: Cambridge University Press.

McGinn, Anne Platt. 1998. "Promoting Sustainable Fisheries." In *State of the World 1998,* ed. Linda Starke. New York: W.W. Norton.

Meozzi, Paolo G. June 5, 1999. Personal interview. European Environment Agency. Copenhagen.

Milner, Henry. 2000. *Civic Literacy.* Hanover and London: Tufts University/University Press of New England.

Ministry of Agriculture, Fisheries and Food (MAFF). 1993. *Solving the Nitrate Problem: Progress in Research and Development.* London: Ministry of Agriculture, Fisheries and Food.

———. 2001. "The First Decisions on Annex I Inclusion." Pesticide Safety Directorate, http://www.pesticides.gov.uk/ec_process/ECreviews/EC%20decisions/ec_decisions. htm.

Moe, Terry M., and Michael Caldwell. 1994. "The Institutional Foundations of Democratic Government: A Comparison of Presidential and Parliamentary Systems." *Journal of Institutional and Theoretical Economics* 150(1):171–195.

Molterer, Wilhelm. 1997. *Making Growth in Organic Trade a Priority.* (Address of the Federal Minister Mag. Molterer.) Conference Proceedings of the 5th IFOAM International Conference on Trade in Organic Products. Christ Church College, Oxford. September 24–27.

Moyer, Wayne, and Tim Josling. 1990. *Agricultural Policy Reform: Politics and Process in the USA and EC.* New York: Harvester Wheatsheaf.

———. 2002. *Agricultural Policy Reform: Politics and Process in the EU and US in the 1990s.* Vermont: Ashgate.

Nelson, Randy A., Tom Tietenberg, and Michael R. Donihue. 1993. "Differential Environmental Regulation: Effects on Electric Utility Capital Turnover and Emissions." *Review of Economics and Statistics* 72 (2):368–373.

Ockenden, Jonathan, and Michael Franklin. 1995. *European Agriculture: Making the CAP Fit the Future.* London: Royal Institute of International Affairs, Chatham House Papers, Pinter Publishers.

OECD. 1985. *Environmental Data: Compendium 1985.* Paris: Organisation for Economic Co-operation and Development.

———. 1986. *Water Pollution by Fertilizers and Pesticide.* Paris: Organisation for Economic Co-operation and Development.

————. 1987. *Environmental Data: Compendium* 1987. Paris: Organisation for Economic Co-operation and Development.

————. 1989. *Environmental Data: Compendium* 1989. Paris: Organisation for Economic Co-operation and Development.

————. 1991. *Environmental Data: Compendium* 1991. Paris: Organisation for Economic Co-operation and Development.

————. 1993a. *Environmental Data: Compendium* 1993. Paris: Organisation for Economic Co-operation and Development.

————. 1993b. *Environmental Performance Reviews: Germany.* Paris: Organisation for Economic Co-operation and Development.

————. 1993c. *Taxation and the Environment: Complementary Policies.* Paris: Organisation for Economic Co-operation and Development.

————. 1994a. *Environmental Performance Reviews: United Kingdom.* Paris: Organisation for Economic Co-operation and Development.

————. 1994b. *The Distributive Effects of Economic Instruments for Environmental Policy.* Paris: Organisation for Economic Co-operation and Development.

————. 1995a. *Agricultural Policy Reform and Adjustment: The Swedish Experience.* Paris: Organisation for Economic Co-operation and Development.

————. 1995b. *Environmental Data: Compendium* 1995. Paris: Organisation for Economic Co-operation and Development.

————. 1995c. *Environmental Performance Reviews: Austria.* Paris: Organisation for Economic Co-operation and Development.

————. 1996. *Environmental Performance Reviews: Sweden.* Paris: Organisation for Economic Co-operation and Development.

————. 1997a. *Environmental Data: Compendium* 1997. Paris: Organisation for Economic Co-operation and Development.

————. 1997b. *Evaluating Economic Instruments for Environmental Policy.* Paris: Organisation for Economic Co-operation and Development.

————. 1999. *Environmental Data: Compendium* 1999. Paris: Organisation for Economic Co-operation and Development.

OECD Environment Directorate. 1996. *Activities to Reduce Pesticide Risks in OECD and Selected FAO Countries, Part I: Summary Report, Part II: Survey Responses.* Paris: Organisation for Economic Co-operation and Development.

Olson, Mancur. 1971. *The Logic of Collective Action.* Cambridge: Harvard University Press.

————. 1982. *The Rise and Decline of Nations: Economic Growth, Stagflation, and Social Rigidities.* New Haven: Yale University Press.

Olsson, Karl Erik. February 4, 1999. Personal interview. Member of the European Parliament. Brussels.

ÖPUL (Austrian Program for Environmental Agriculture). N.d. (c. 1996). *Overview of National and Regional Support Policies for Agriculture, the Food Industry and the Rural Areas.* Vienna: Federal Ministry of Agriculture and Forestry.

O'Riorden, Tim. March 3, 1999. Personal interview. Centre for Social and Economic Research on the Global Environment, University of East Anglia, Norwich.

Pappi, Franz U., and Christian H. C. A. Henning. "The Organization of Influence on the ECs Common Agricultural Policy: A Network Approach." 1999. *European Journal of Political Research* 36:257–281.

Parkin, Sara. 1989. *Green Parties: An International Guide.* London: Heretic Books.

Pehle, Henrich. 1997. "Germany: Domestic Obstacles to an International Forerunner." In *European Environmental Policy: The Pioneers,* ed. Mikael Skou Anderson and Duncan Liefferink. Oxford: Manchester University Press.

Persson, Torsten, and Guido Tabellini. 1999. "The Size and Scope of Government: Comparative Politics with Rational Politics. 1998 Alfred Marshall Lecture." *European Economic Review* 43:699–735.

———. 2000. "Comparative Politics and Public Finance." *Journal of Political Economy* 108:1121–1161.

———. 2005. *The Economic Effects of Constitutions.* Cambridge, Mass.: MIT Press.

Pesticide Section of the National Centre for Ecotoxicology and Hazardous Substances. 1999. *Pesticides in the Aquatic Environment.* Wallingford: Environment Agency.

Pesticides Forum. 1999. *Pesticides Forum Annual Report* 1998. London: Ministry of Agriculture, Fisheries and Food.

Pettersson, Olle. 1993. "Swedish Pesticide Policy in a Changing Environment." In *The Pesticide Question: Environment, Economics, and Ethics,* ed. David Pimentel and Hugh Lehman. New York: Chapman and Hall.

———. 1997. "Pesticide Use in Swedish Agriculture: The Case of a 75% Reduction." In *Techniques for Reducing Pesticide Use,* ed. D. Pimentel. Chichester, U.K.: John Wiley.

Pierson, Paul. 1995. "Fragmented Welfare States: Federal Institutions and the Development of Social Policy." *Governance.* 449–478.

Pierson, Paul D., and R. Kent Weaver. 1993. "Imposing Losses in Pension Policy." In *Do Institutions Matter? Government Capabilities in the United States and Abroad,* ed. R. Kent Weaver and Bert A. Rockman, 110–150. Washington, D.C.: Brookings Institution.

Porter, Clive. 1999. Personal interview. Reader in European Rural Policy, Wye College. Kent.

Porter, Gareth, Janet Brown, and Pamela S. Chasek. 2010. *Global Environmental Politics.* Boulder: Westview Press.

Posch, Alois. April 26, 1999. Personal interview. Federal Ministry of Agriculture and Forestry. Vienna.

Powell, G. Bingham. 1982. *Contemporary Democracies: Participation, Stability, and Violence.* Cambridge, Mass.: Harvard University Press.

———. 2000. *Elections as Instruments of Democracy.* New Haven: Yale University Press.

———. 2004. "The Chain of Responsiveness." *Journal of Democracy* 15 (4):91–105.

Powell, G. Bingham, and Guy D. Whitten. 1993. "A Cross-National Analysis of Economic Voting: Taking Account of the Political Context." *American Journal of Political Science* 37 (2):391–414.

Powick, Jane, Antony Williamson, and Nick Zamen. March 5, 1999. Personal interview. The National Centre for Ecotoxicology and Hazardous Substances, U.K. Environment Agency. Wallingford, England.

Press, Daniel. 1994. *Democratic Dilemmas in the Age of Ecology*. Durham: Duke University Press.

Quattrone, George, and Amos Tverskey. 1988. "Contrasting Rational and Psychological Analysis of Political Choice." *American Political Science Review* 82:719–736.

Rapsomanikis, George. 1999. Personal interview. Centre for European Agricultural Studies, Wye College. Kent.

Reynolds, Andrew. 1996. "The Curious Case of Afghanistan." *Journal of Democracy* 17 (2):104–117.

Riker, William H. 1982. *Liberalism Against Populism*. San Francisco: W. H. Freeman.

Rillearts, Francis. January 25, 1999. Personal interview. The Union of European Water Undertakers (EUREAU). Brussels.

Rogowski, Ronald, and Mark Andreas Kayser. 2002. "Majoritarian Electoral System and Consumer Power." *American Journal of Political Science* 46 (3):526–539.

Roller, Edeltraud. 2005. *The Performance of Democracies*. Oxford: Oxford University Press.

Rootes, Chris. 1995. "Britain: Greens in a Cold Climate." In *The Green Challenge: The Development of Green Parties in Europe,* ed. Dick Richardson and Chris Rootes. London: Routledge.

Rose, Richard. 1983. "Elections and Electoral Systems: Choices and Alternatives." In *Democracy and Elections,* ed. Vernon Bogdanor and David Butler. Cambridge: Cambridge University Press.

Rothchild, Donald, and Philip G. Roeder. 2000. *The Role of Power Sharing in Designing Stable Democracies*. Paper delivered at the Conference on Powersharing and Peacemaking, La Jolla. December 8–9.

Rudquist, Gun. June 8, 1999. Personal interview. Officer of Agriculture, Swedish Society for Nature Conservation. Stockholm, Sweden.

Sakamoto, Takayuki. 2008. *Economic Policy and Performance in Industrial Democracies: Party Governments, Central Banks and the Fiscal-monetary Policy Mix*. New York: Routledge.

Samuels, David J. 2002. "Pork Barreling Is Not Credit Claiming or Advertising: Campaign Finance and the Sources of the Personal Vote in Brazil." *Journal of Politics* 64 (3):845–862.

———. 2004. "Presidentialism and Accountability for the Economy in Comparative Perspective." *American Political Science Review* 98 (3):425–436.

Samuels, David J., and Matthew Soberg Shugart. 2003. "Presidentialism, Elections and Representation." *Journal of Theoretical Politics* 15 (1):22–60.

Schattschneider, E. E. 1960. *The Semisovereign People; A Realist's View of Democracy in America*. New York: Holt, Rinehart and Winston.

Scheierling, Susanne M. 1995. *Overcoming Agricultural Pollution of Water: The Challenge of Integrating Agricultural and Environmental Policies in the European Union*. World Bank Technical Paper Number 269. Washington D.C.: The World Bank.

Schmidt, Manfred G. 1996. "When Parties Matter: A Review of the Possibilities and Limits of Partisan Influence on Public Policy." *European Journal of Political Research* 30:155–183.

———. 1997. "Determinants of Social Expenditure in Liberal Democracies: The Post World War II Experience." *Acta Politica* 32 (3):153–173.

Schmitter, Philippe C. 1974. "Still the Century of Corporatism?" In *The New Corporatism,* ed. Fredrick B. Pike and Thomas Stritch. Notre Dame: University of Notre Dame Press.

———. 2004. "The Ambiguous Virtues of Accountability." *Journal of Democracy* 15 (4):47–60.

Schulz, Dietrich. June 1, 1999. Personal interview. Federal Environmental Agency. Berlin.

Schumpeter, J. 1954. *Capitalism, Socialism, and Democracy.* London: Allen and Unwin.

Schwaiger, Karl. April 28, 1999. Personal interview. Federal Ministry of Agriculture and Forestry. Vienna.

Scruggs, Lyle. 2003. *Sustaining Abundance.* New York: Cambridge University Press.

Shugart, Matthew Soberg. 1996. "Checks and Balances in Latin America: In an Age of Globalization." Unpublished paper.

Shugart, Matthew Soberg, and John Carey. 1992. *Presidents and Assemblies: Constitutional Design and Electoral Dynamics.* Cambridge: Cambridge University Press.

Shugart, Matthew Soberg, and Martin P. Wattenburg. 2001. *Mixed Member Electoral Systems: The Best of Both Worlds?* Oxford: Oxford University Press.

Simmons, Beth. 1994. *Who Adjusts? Domestic Sources of Foreign Economic Policy During the Interwar Years.* Princeton: Princeton University Press.

Simon, Regina A. 1971. "Public Attitudes Toward Population and Pollution." *Public Opinion Quarterly* 35:95–102.

Stamm, Keith R., Fiona Clark, and Paula Reynolds Eblacas. 2000. "Mass Communication and Public Understanding of Environmental Problems: The Case of Global Warming." *Public Understanding of Science* 9:219–237.

Steinmo, Sven. 1989. "Political Institutions and Tax Policy." *World Politics* 41 (4):500–535.

Steinmo, Sven, and Caroline J. Tolbert. 1998. "Do Institutions Really Matter? Taxation in Industrialized Democracies." *Comparative Political Studies* 31 (2):165–187.

Steinmo, Sven, and Jon Watts. 1995. "It's the Institutions, Stupid! Why Comprehensive National Health Insurance Always Fails in America." *Journal of Health Politics Policy and Law* 20 (2):329–372.

Stone-Sweet, Alec. 2004. *The Judicial Construction of Europe.* Oxford: Oxford University Press.

Strøm, Kaare. 1984. "Minority Governments in Parliamentary Democracies." *Comparative Political Studies* 17:199–227.

———. 1985. "Party Goals and Government Performance in Parliamentary Democracies." *American Political Science Review* 79 (3):738–754.

————. 1990. *Minority Government and Majority Rule.* Cambridge: Cambridge University Press.

Strøm, Kaare, and Wolfgang C. Müller. 2009. "Parliamentary Democracy, Agency Problem and Party Politics." In *Intra-party Politics and Government Coalitions,* ed. Daniela Giannetti and Kenneth Benoit. Oxon: Routledge.

Strøm, Kaare, and Steve Swindle. 1993. "Political Parties, Institutions and Environmental Reform." Working Paper 2.17. University of California Center for German and European Studies, Berkeley, Calif.

Svedinger, Ingrid. June 9, 1999. Personal interview. Ministry of Agriculture. Stockholm.

Swan, Shanna S. H., C. Brazil, E. Z. Drobnis, F. Liu, R. L. Kruse, M. Hatch, J. Bruce Redmon, C. Wang, and J. W. Overstreet. 2003. "Geographic Differences in Semen Quality of Fertile US Males." *Environmental Health Perspectives* 111.

Thomas, Miles. March 4, 1999. Personal Interview. Head of Pesticide Usage Surveys, Central Science Laboratory, Ministry of Agriculture, Fisheries and Food. York.

Tracy, Michael. 1996. *Agriculture Policy in the European Union.* Genappe-La Hutte: APS-Agricultural Policy Studies.

Tsebelis, George. 1995a. "Decision Making in Political Systems: Veto Players in Presidentialism, Multicameralism and Multipartyism." *British Journal of Political Science* 25:289–325.

————. 1995b. "Veto Players and Law Production in Parliamentary Democracies." In *Parliaments and Majority Rule in Western Europe,* ed. Herbert Doring. New York: St. Martin's Press.

————. 2002. *Veto Players: How Political Institutions Work.* Princeton: Princeton University Press.

United Nations Food and Agriculture Organization (FAO). 2000. FAOSTAT Database Collections. fao.org/page/collections?subset=agriculture.

United Nations Statistical Commission and Economic Commission for Europe Conference of European Statisticians Statistical Standards and Studies 42. 1992. *The Environment in Europe and North America: Annotated Statistics 1992.* New York: United Nations.

Vail, David, Knut Per Hasund, and Lars Drake. 1994. *The Greening of Agricultural Policies in Industrial Societies: Swedish Reforms in Comparative Perspective.* Ithaca, N.Y.: Cornell University Press.

van der Bijl, Gert, Henk van Zeijts, and Karlheinz Knickel. 1999. "Nitrogen Problems and Current Policies." In *Economic Instruments for Nitrogen Control in European Agriculture,* ed. H. Van Zeijts. Utrecht: Centre for Agriculture and Environment (CLM).

van Zeijts, Henk, ed. 1999. *Economic Instruments for Nitrogen Control in European Agriculture.* Utrecht: Centre for Agriculture and Environment (CLM).

Verba, Sidney, Kay Lehaman Scholzman, and Henry Brady. 1995. *Voice and Equality.* Cambridge: Harvard University Press.

Vig, Norman J., and Michael E. Kraft, eds. 1994. *Environmental Policy in the 1990s.* 2d ed. Washington D.C.: CQ Press.

Vlahodimos, Konstantinos P. January 19, 1999. Personal interview. Global Crop Protection Federation. Brussels.

Vogel, David. 1987. *National Styles of Regulation*. Ithaca, N.Y.: Cornell University Press.

———. 1993. "Representing Diffuse Interests in Environmental Policymaking." In *Do Institutions Matter? Government Capabilities in the United States and Abroad,* ed. R. Kent Weaver and Bert A. Rockman. Washington D.C.: Brookings Institution.

von Krocher, Carolin. May 24, 1999. Personal interview. Agricultural Chamber of Hannover. Hannover.

Vorreyer, Christian. May 18, 1999. Personal interview. Ministry of Agriculture. Bonn, Germany.

Wachendorfer-Schmidt, Ute. 2000. *Federalism and Political Performance*. New York: Routledge.

Wallace, W. 1996. *Policymaking in the European Union*. Oxford: Oxford University Press.

Watelet, Nathalie. 1999. Personal interview. Manager, Agriculture and Environment, European Crop protection Association. Brussels.

Weale, Albert. 1992. *The New Politics of Pollution*. Manchester and New York: Manchester University Press.

Weaver, R. Kent, and Bert A. Rockman, eds. 1993. *Do Institutions Matter? Government Capabilities in the United States and Abroad.* Washington D.C.: Brookings Institution.

———. 1993. "Assessing the Effects of Institutions." *In Do Institutions Matter? Government Capabilities in the United States and Abroad,* ed. R. Kent Weaver and Bert A. Rockman, 1–41. Washington, D.C.: Brookings Institution.

———. 1993. "Institutional Reform and Constitutional Design." In *Do Institutions Matter? Government Capabilities in the United States and Abroad,* ed. R. Kent Weaver and Bert A. Rockman. Washington D.C.: Brookings Institution.

Weingarten, Peter. 1997. *Agri-Environmental Policy in Germany: Soil and Water Conservation. Discussion Paper No. 4*. Halle: Institute of Agricultural Development in Central and Eastern Europe.

White, Brian. 2001. *Understanding European Foreign Policy*. New York: Palgrave.

Winter, Michael. 1996. *Rural Politics*. London: Routledge.

Wise, Christopher. February 25, 1999. Personal interview. National Farmers Union. London.

Wolf. 1999. Personal interview. Bonn.

Young, K. 1987. "Interim Report: The Countryside." In *British Social Attitudes: The 1987 Report,* ed. R. Jowell, S. Witherspoon, and L. Brook. Aldershot, U.K.: Grover.

———. 1989. "Interim Report: Rural Prospects." In *British Social Attitudes: The 5th Report,* ed. R. Jowell, S. Witherspoon, and L. Brook. Aldershot, U.K.: Grover.

INDEX

Tables (*t*) and notes (*n*) are indicated following page numbers.